THE AUSTRALIAN
Women's Weekly

easy PARTY CAKES

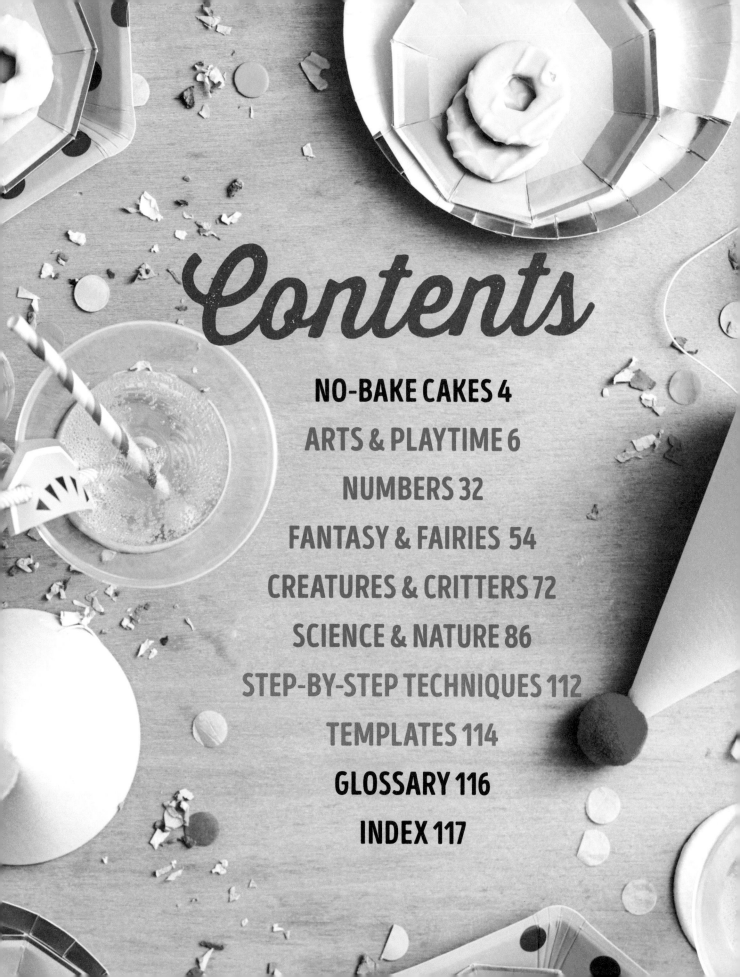

Contents

NO-BAKE CAKES

If you have a child about to celebrate a birthday you're probably wondering where you're going to find the time to bake and decorate a cake and arrange a party. Well, wonder no more: The Australian Women's Weekly is here to help with *Easy Party Cakes*.

The praise we've received from readers for our previous two cookbooks in this easy party cake series, *Cheat's Cakes* and *Cheat's Cakes 2*, has been so positive that we've gone back to the kitchen to create more fabulous cakes for a third book.

As with our other easy party cake books, we make good use of pre-made cakes and other products found in the supermarket bakery section. And that's the secret – buy basic store-bought cakes and other baked goods, don't bake them. No need to weigh, measure, beat or wait for the oven to heat up – all the hard work is done; simply ice the cake and apply the decorations, it's that easy.

Thank goodness for today's well-stocked supermarkets. They are a boon for busy mums and dads, and this is never more true than when it comes time to make and decorate the yearly birthday cake, or cakes, as the case often is. And it seems that more and more of us are taking advantage of the fantastic collection of cake decorating items on offer in-store.

The supermarket confectionery and baking aisles are an Aladdin's Cave of ready-made icings, frostings, writing gels, fondants, sugar decorations, sprinkles, sparkles, chocolate buttons, lollies, sugar pearls and more, and the selection of colours and shapes is amazing.

The bakery section has a great selection of pre-made square and round cakes, doughnuts, cupcakes, jam rolls, muffins and lamingtons – everything you need to put together your child's chosen cake is available here.

The cake designs the Test Kitchen team created really are amazing – they are, mostly, minimum fuss, and all have maximum impact. Kids will love the variety to choose from. There are simple

number cakes for the littlies; cakes for up-and-coming chefs, farmers and market gardeners; cakes for budding scientists and explorers; and animal cakes. There are even quirky 'fruit cakes' – including a fruit 'pizza' and a fruit 'desert island'!

To make the most of these recipes, a little planning is necessary – you need to read the recipe right through before starting your shopping list. Some of the cakes may need to set or freeze for a couple of hours or overnight, so you need to work out when you are going to decorate the cake, and how long it will take. Some of the cakes are fiddly – they're not all that hard, but they do require a bit of extra time and patience – however, the end result is well worth it. And, the fantastic pictures alongside each recipe means you can see at a glance how your finished cake should look. Remember, regardless of whether the cake looks picture perfect, or a bit lop-sided or rough and ready (and we've all been there), your child will love it.

At the back of the book are helpful tips on melting chocolate, preparing cakes for decorating, covering cake boards and making piping bags. However, if you want to cheat a little more, use a ziptop bag as a piping bag, and buy pre-covered cake boards from supermarkets, major department stores and cake decorating suppliers – we're all for anything that makes life simpler!

Another trick of the trade to add further 'wow' factor to your child's cake, is the additional toys and backgrounds that will lift the look of the cake as it is presented at the table. Look at the pictures of our cakes, and then use cardboard, sparkles, straws, balloons, small toys, etc., from craft stores, discount stores, newsagents and toy stores to add a whole other dimension to the cake.

These days we may be pressed for time, and the cakes may be put together a little differently, but our kids are sure to remember these birthday cakes just as fondly as we remember our own.

ARTS & PLAYTIME

TIP *Choose any colours you like for the candles, and match the frosting to them.*

MELTED CANDLE CAKE

TAKES UNDER 1 HOUR

EQUIPMENT

30cm x 40cm (12-inch x 16-inch)
rectangular cake board (page 112)

CAKE

1 x 450g (14½-ounce) packaged
double unfilled sponge cake slabs

3 x 453g (14½-ounce) tubs vanilla
frosting

DECORATIONS

assorted coloured candles (we used
purple, yellow, pink, green)

assorted food colouring to match
candle colours

1   Secure one cake to cake board with a little frosting; spread top of cake with 2 tablespoons of frosting. Top with remaining cake. Trim edges.

2   Divide 2 tubs of frosting evenly into 4 small microwave-safe bowls; tint each with one of the colours to match the colour of the candles. Spread the remaining tub of plain frosting over the top and sides of the cake.

3   Microwave one of the coloured frostings on HIGH (100%) for 20 seconds or until melted. Pour frosting, in patches, over top and edges of cake to resemble melted wax. Repeat using remaining frosting. Place coloured candles into the 'melted candle wax' frosting.

TIP *Make sure you remove the toothpicks before serving.*

FRUIT SALAD TOWER

TAKES UNDER 1 HOUR

EQUIPMENT

25cm (10-inch) round cake board (page 112) or a flat-based coloured plastic container

melon baller

30 toothpicks

MELON BASE

4kg (8-pound) whole round seedless watermelon

2kg (4-pound) whole rockmelon

DECORATIONS

1kg (2-pound) honeydew melon, seeds scraped

2 kiwifruit, peeled, quartered

1 Trim both ends off the watermelon, leaving a 15cm (6-inch) wide middle section with two flat ends. Slice off skin around all sides to create eight even flat edges. Place in centre of cake board or on an upturned flat-based container. (The upturned container gives the fruit tower a little extra height.)

2 Trim ends off rockmelon, leaving a 12cm (4¾-inch) wide middle section with two flat ends. Scoop out seeds with a spoon. Slice off skin around all sides to create eight even flat edges. Arrange rockmelon on top of watermelon so the edges of the rockmelon are slightly at an angle to the edges of the watermelon.

3 Scoop melon balls from honeydew melon. Cut 15 of the honeydew balls in half. Insert a toothpick halfway into the ball from the flat side, then push skewer into watermelon. Repeat to create a polka dot pattern on the watermelon.

4 Top rockmelon with the remaining honeydew balls and kiwifruit, piling the fruit inside the rockmelon centre.

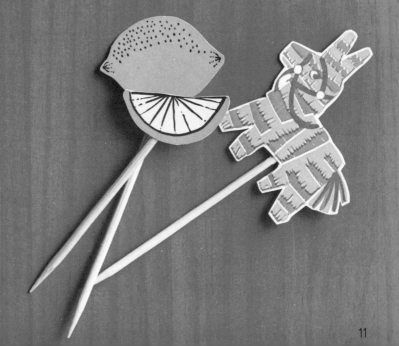

11

TO MARKET, TO MARKET

TAKES UNDER 1 HOUR

EQUIPMENT

30cm x 40cm (12-inch x 16-inch) rectangular cake board (page 112)

CAKE

1 x 450g (14½-ounce) packaged double unfilled sponge cake slabs

1 x 453g (14½-ounce) tub chocolate frosting

1 x 12cm (4¾-inch) packaged long jam sponge roll, halved lengthways

DECORATIONS

5 ice-cream wafers, halved lengthways

180g (5½-ounce) packet Starburst Fruitful Mix

8 green gumballs

100g (3 ounces) white chocolate Melts, plus 4 extra

2 chocolate cream-filled biscuits, halved, filling removed

5cm (2-inch) piece white musk stick, halved lengthways

12cm (4¾-inch) piece licorice strap

2 white round mints

2 each yellow and orange Smarties

2 yellow mini M&M's

14 blue mini M&M's

2 x 5cm (2-inch) pieces blue musk sticks, halved lengthways, then halved crossways

1 rainbow strap

1 chocolate malt stick biscuit

1 Trim one cake so it is 12cm (4¾-inch) wide; secure to cake board with a little frosting. Trim remaining cake into a 12cm (4¾-inch) square; stand upright to form front cabin of the truck, securing with a little frosting. Press one jam roll half onto front of truck; secure with a little frosting if necessary (discard or reserve remaining half for another use).

2 Spread frosting over top and sides of cake.

3 Press two wafers into each side of truck, trimming to fit length of truck. Press one wafer into back of truck for tailgate. Press remaining wafers into the middle of the truck, trimming to fit, to form containers for the fruit.

4 Fill wafer 'fruit' containers with lolly fruits and gumballs.

5 Melt the 100g chocolate (page 113). Using a little of the melted chocolate, attach extra chocolate Melts to biscuits for hub caps. Secure biscuits on cake for wheels.

6 Trim one white musk stick half into a flat rectangle (discard remaining half). Using picture as a guide, use melted chocolate to secure musk stick half to the centre of the licorice strap; secure mints on either side. Position and secure yellow Smarties onto mints for headlights. Secure licorice strap 'bumper bar' to cake.

7 Using picture as a guide, decorate cake with remaining lollies, trimming to fit as necessary. Position biscuit stick for the exhaust pipe.

FRUITY MUFFINS

Each recipe decorates 4 muffins. We used a 420g (13½-ounce) package of 4 muffins.

APPLE OF MY EYE

TAKES UNDER 1 HOUR

Cut a small cone-shaped hollow from the centre of 4 choc-chip muffins. Tint half a 453g (14½-ounce) tub of vanilla frosting red. Spread frosting over tops of muffins. Cut 2 pretzel sticks in half. Dip pretzel sticks into 50g (1½-ounces) melted milk chocolate Melts (page 113). Place on baking paper to set. Cut 2 spearmint leaves in half lengthways. Position spearmint leaves and pretzel sticks into the centre of each apple.

SPIKY PINEAPPLE

TAKES UNDER 1 HOUR

Trim and discard the tops off 4 choc-chip muffins. Tint half a 453g (14½-ounce) tub of vanilla frosting yellow. Spread frosting over top of muffins. Discard the green part from 1½ cups of pineapple lollies. Position pineapple lollies over tops of muffins. Using scissors, cut 4 spearmint leaves in half lengthways then, without cutting all the way through, cut into thin strips lengthwise to make pineapple tops. Press into top of each muffin.

EACH RECIPE DECORATES 4 MUFFINS

WATTA MELON!

TAKES UNDER 1 HOUR

Trim tops off 4 choc-chip muffins; reserve tops. Cut cake tops into wedge shapes. Divide half a 453g (14½-ounce) tub of vanilla frosting into two bowls. Tint one green, leave the remaining bowl plain. Ice top of each muffin with green frosting. Spread white frosting over wedge shapes. Cut 8 semi-circle shapes from 4 extreme red sour straps; press onto sides of wedges. Cut green part from 4 rainbow sour straps and secure around base of each wedge. Cut 12 brown mini M&M's in half crossways, secure 3 halves to each side of wedge with plain frosting.

NOT-SO-SOUR GRAPES

TAKES UNDER 1 HOUR

Trim and discard the tops off 4 choc-chip muffins. Tint half a 453g (14½-ounce) tub of vanilla frosting purple. Spread frosting over tops of muffins. Dip 4 pretzel sticks into 50g (1½-ounces) melted milk chocolate Melts (page 113). Place on baking paper to set. Insert a pretzel stick into the centre of each muffin, trimming to fit. Using 1½ cups purple berry lollies, stack lollies around pretzel sticks. Split 2 spearmint leaves in half lengthways; position one half on top of 'grapes' beside pretzels.

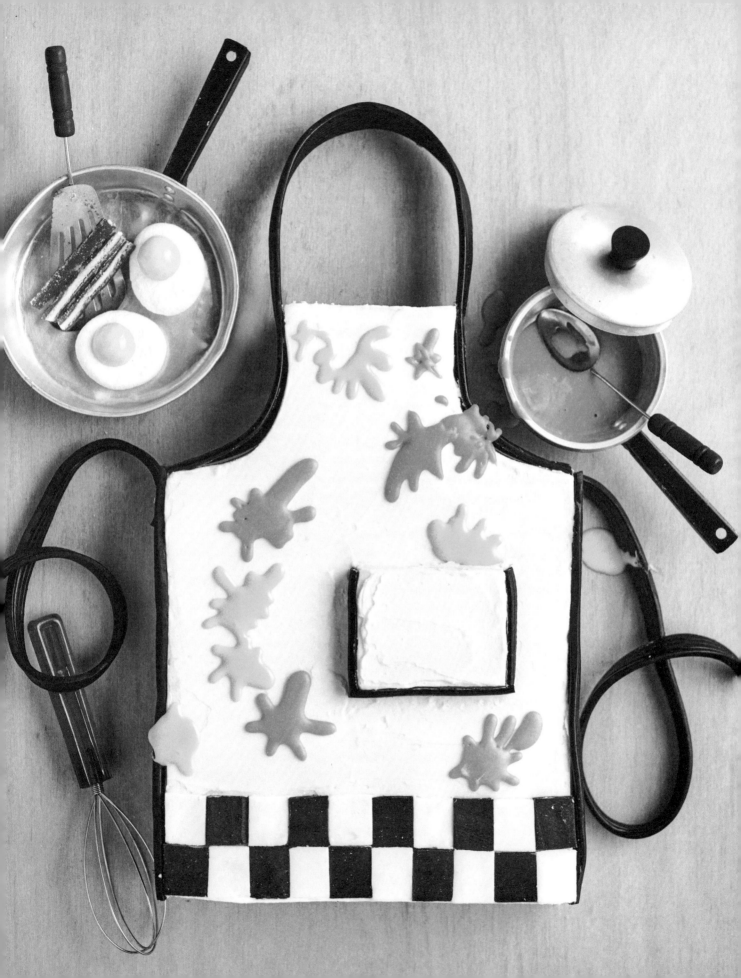

MESSY CHEF'S APRON

TAKES UNDER 1 HOUR

EQUIPMENT

30cm x 40cm (12-inch x 16-inch) rectangular cake board (page 112)

10cm (4-inch) round cutter

CAKE

1 x 450g (14½-ounce) packaged double unfilled sponge cake slabs

1 x 453g (14½-ounce) tub vanilla frosting

DECORATIONS

1 jam rollette

2 x 1-metre (1-yard) pieces black licorice strap

10 licorice allsorts

green and yellow food colouring

small toy kitchen utensils

1 Secure one cake to cake board with a little frosting. Using picture as a guide, and using the round cutter, trim edges from remaining cake to form top of apron. Secure to cake board with a little frosting, ensuring cakes line up in an apron shape.

2 Reserve ½ cup frosting. Spread remaining frosting over top and sides of cake.

3 Carefully unroll jam rollette; trim into a 5cm x 7cm (2-inch x 2¾-inch) rectangle. Place on cake to make a pocket. Cover with 2 tablespoons of the reserved frosting, then outline with a little of the licorice strap, cutting to fit around pocket.

4 Slice licorice allsorts into layers; reserve black and white pieces (discard remaining coloured slices). Arrange black and white squares on apron in a chequerboard pattern.

5 Wrap the remaining licorice strap around the sides of the cake to form the neck and waist straps of the apron, cutting to fit.

6 Divide remaining frosting into 2 microwave-safe bowls; tint green and yellow. Microwave on HIGH (100%) for 20 seconds or until melted. Splatter frosting over apron.

7 Arrange kitchen utensils around cake.

TIP Unroll the licorice strap and leave overnight to straighten the strap.

TIP Serve with pineapple 'chips' (fries); simply cut slices of fresh pineapple into chip shapes, about 1cm (½-inch) thick.

FRUIT PIZZA

TAKES UNDER 1 HOUR

EQUIPMENT

2 x 25cm (10-inch) round
cake boards (page 112)

CAKE

2 x 16cm (6½-inch) diameter
rounds rockmelon, cut 1cm
(½-inch) thick, peeled

2 x 14cm (5½-inch) diameter
rounds seedless watermelon,
cut 1cm (½-inch) thick, peeled

DECORATIONS

50g (1½-ounce) piece fresh
pineapple, peeled, cut into
matchsticks

4 strawberries, hulled, sliced
crossways

14 blueberries

1 kiwifruit, peeled, sliced, cut into
small wedges

1   Discard seeds from centre of rockmelon slices; position slices on cake boards.

2   Top rockmelon with watermelon then with remaining ingredients to resemble a pizza.

TIPS Any colourful fruit can be used as a 'pizza topping', although fruit that browns when cut, such as apples, pears and bananas, should not be used unless the pizza is served immediately. The pizza can be assembled up to 3 hours ahead, store in the refrigerator.

TIP *If your kids don't like licorice, swap the strap on the ramp with grey-tinted vanilla frosting and replace the allsorts tiles with Starburst Chews.*

SKATEBOARD RAMP

TAKES OVER 1 HOUR

EQUIPMENT

20cm x 35cm (8-inch x 14-inch) rectangular cake board (page 112)

CAKE

2 x 453g (14½-ounce) tubs vanilla frosting

yellow food colouring

2 x 450g (14½-ounce) packaged double unfilled sponge cake slabs

DECORATIONS

2 x 120g (4-ounce) packets black licorice straps

2 x 240g (7½-ounce) packets licorice allsorts

16 thick ice-cream wafers

4 Fizzers

16 assorted coloured mini M&M's

1 Tint frosting yellow. Cut one cake slab in half crossways; secure 1½ cake slabs, short sides together on the cake board with a little frosting to create a long rectangle. Halve whole slabs crossways and position upright on cake at each end to make ramp walls; secure with a little frosting. Cut remaining cake piece in half and secure to the inside of the cake 'walls' to make two shorter 'walls'. Using a serrated knife, cut a rounded ramp shape from cake, leaving a 3cm (1¼-inch) edge on either side for ramp walls. Reserve any cake trimmings, and place over the base of the ramp to build it up a little.

2 Spread frosting all over cake using generous amounts over the base and up the sides of the walls to make the rounded ramp shape.

3 Using picture as a guide, measure and trim licorice straps to cover inside surface of ramp; arrange side by side, pressing gently into frosting to secure, then place 2 pieces across the top to finish. Slice licorice allsorts into individual coloured tiles. Press tiles in a chequered pattern along both sides of ramp.

4 Trim and press wafers for 'safety fence' on outside and across the top of the cake. Using scissors, trim ends of each Fizzer into a rounded edge to create a skateboard. Press M&M's into sides of boards. Position skateboards on ramp.

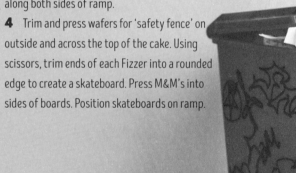

SANDY CASTLE HIDEAWAY

TAKES OVER 1 HOUR (+ STANDING & REFRIGERATION)

EQUIPMENT

30cm x 40cm (12-inch x 16-inch) rectangular cake board (page 112)

6cm (2½-inch) round cutter

1 small disposable piping bag

12 toothpicks

CAKE

2 x 450g (14½-ounce) packaged double unfilled sponge cake slabs

1½ x 453g (14½-ounce) tubs vanilla frosting

DECORATIONS

250g (8-ounce) packet milk arrowroot biscuits

150g (4½ ounces) white chocolate Melts

5 waffle ice-cream cones

5 flag cake toppers

1 malt biscuit

6 pink soft fruit salad jelly wedges

1 round orange jube, halved

1 pink meringue

2 white tangfastic marshmallows

6 brown mini M&M's

3 mini pink marshmallows, halved

mini pink Smarties and purple choc rocks

1 Spread tops of 2 cakes with a little frosting and top each with one of the unfrosted cakes. Cut one cake stack in half crossways, then split one of the halved cakes back into single layers. Cut the single cake layers into 4 x 6cm (2½-inch) circles using the cutter.

2 Blend or process biscuits to make fine crumbs. Pour onto a tray lined with baking paper.

3 Spread tops and sides of the four cake circles with a thin layer of frosting; press into crushed biscuits to evenly coat all over. Spread sides of the larger cakes with a little frosting; press in crushed biscuits to evenly coat all over (page 112). Spread tops of cakes with a little frosting; press biscuit crumbs over cake tops. Stand at room temperature for 1 hour or until firm enough to handle.

4 Meanwhile, melt chocolate (page 113); fill piping bag with melted chocolate. Pipe coral shapes on a sheet of baking paper. Refrigerate until set.

5 Using a little of the remaining frosting, secure the large cake piece to the cake board. Dollop a little frosting in the centre of the cake top, then top with the smaller cake. Position the round cake pieces at the front and on either side of the cake; secure with a little frosting. Push an upturned waffle cone into each round cake piece and one on top of the cake. Push flags into top of cones. Position malt biscuit for door.

6 Using picture as a guide, insert toothpicks into one end of fruit wedges and jube halves. Insert 2 wedges into the sides of meringue and white marshmallows for claws. Using a little melted chocolate, secure mini M&M's to mini marshmallows to make 'eyes'. Secure 2 sets of eyes onto toothpicks and one set onto jubes. Insert toothpicks into top of meringue and marshmallows to complete the crabs.

7 Scatter any remaining biscuit crumbs over and around castle. Place chocolate coral, Smarties and choc rocks around castle. Place crabs on and around castle, as pictured.

TIP Be sure to remove toothpicks before serving.

HOT DIGGITY DOGS

TAKES UNDER 1 HOUR (+ STANDING)

EQUIPMENT

1 small disposable piping bag

CAKE

1 x 400g (12½-ounce) packaged madeira cake

6 fruit-filled oven baked fruit bars

1 x 453g (14½-ounce) tub vanilla frosting

red and yellow food colouring

1 x 250g (8-ounce) packaged 6 mini jam sponge rolls

1 Cut madeira cake into 1cm (½-inch) thick x 6cm (2½-inch) long 'chips'.

2 Remove fruit bars from packaging and place on a wire rack over a sheet of baking paper.

3 Place three-quarters of the frosting in a microwave-safe bowl; tint red. Tint remaining frosting yellow.

4 Microwave red frosting for 20 seconds on HIGH (100%) or until melted. Pour red frosting over fruit bars to completely cover; stand 'frankfurts' at room temperature for 30 minutes or until firm enough to handle.

5 Cut jam rolls in half lengthways, leaving a single layer of sponge attached at the base. Insert frankfurts into jam rolls. Fill piping bag with yellow frosting; drizzle the 'mustard' onto hotdogs.

6 Microwave any remaining red frosting on HIGH (100%) for 20 seconds and drizzle over chips for 'sauce'.

SHAKE IT UP
Each recipe is enough for 1 serving.

CARAMEL SHAKE

TAKES UNDER 30 MINUTES

Place 4 hard toffee caramel lollies in a large ziptop bag; pound with a rolling pin until coarsely crushed. Dip the rim of a serving jar into 50g (1½ ounces) melted white chocolate (page 113) then dip into crushed toffee caramel. Stand 1½ cups vanilla ice-cream at room temperature for 10 minutes to soften slightly. Swirl 2 tablespoons of caramel sauce through the ice-cream then spoon into serving jar. Thread 1 waffle, 1 mini muffin, 1 party ring biscuit and 1 small doughnut onto a long bamboo skewer. Push skewer into ice-cream. Drizzle with 2 teaspoons caramel sauce and 2 teaspoons chocolate sauce. Top with a chocolate-coated pretzel.

CHERRY BERRY SHAKE

TAKES UNDER 30 MINUTES

Stand 1½ cups berry and lemon sorbet at room temperature for 10 minutes to soften slightly. Drizzle 2 tablespoons strawberry topping down the inside of the serving glass. Spoon sorbet into glass until three-quarters full. Cut 1 fun-sized cherry ripe into 3 pieces lengthways. Thread cherry ripe onto a toothpick or small skewer. Press a maraschino cherry into the top. Top shake with a meringue swirl and the cherry-ripe skewer. Serve drizzled with strawberry topping.

EXTREME CHOC SHAKE

TAKES UNDER 30 MINUTES

Stand 1½ cups chocolate choc-chip ice-cream at room temperature for 10 minutes to soften slightly. Layer ice-cream and ¼ cup chocolate topping in a large serving glass until three-quarters full. Top with a double choc-chip muffin. Top muffin with a swirl of canned whipped cream, then drizzle generously with chocolate topping. Top shake with a chocolate Flake bar and scatter over ½ teaspoon each of dark and white chocolate sprinkles.

RING TOSS

TAKES UNDER 1 HOUR

EQUIPMENT

20cm (8-inch) square cake board
(page 112)

CAKE

1 x 450g (14½-ounce) packaged
double unfilled sponge cake slabs

1 x 453g (14½-ounce) tub vanilla
frosting

DECORATIONS

7 extreme red sour straps

125g (4 ounces) milk arrowroot
biscuits, broken into pieces

green food colouring

20cm (8-inch) piece dowel (new)

5 glazed doughnuts

1 Spread top of one cake with ¼ cup frosting, then top with remaining cake. Trim cake into a cube shape. Secure cake to cake board with a little frosting. Spread remaining frosting all over cake.

2 Position sour straps around base of the cake, trimming to fit as necessary. Cut remaining sour straps into 5mm (¼-inch) thick lengths. Using picture as a guide, make a large square on top of the cake with the sour strap; arrange remaining sour strap into a cross pattern within the square, leaving room for the dowel to be inserted through the centre.

3 Place biscuits and food colouring into a food processor or blender; pulse until the crumbs are evenly coloured; sprinkle crumbs around cake.

4 Insert the dowel through the centre of the cake. Arrange doughnuts on the dowel and around the cake.

HOT AIR BALLOONS

TAKES UP TO 1 HOUR

EQUIPMENT

3 balloons

cooking-oil spray

3 clothes pegs

25cm (10-inch) round cake board (page 112)

6 x 20cm (8-inch) bamboo skewers

CAKE

½ x 453g (14½-ounce) tub vanilla frosting

blue food colouring

1 x 460g (14½-ounce) packaged double unfilled sponge cake rounds

DECORATIONS

375g (12 ounces) white chocolate Melts

various coloured edible confetti sprinkles

3 extreme red sour straps

3 extra thick ice-cream wafers

8 white round mints

1 Melt chocolate (page 113) in a large heatproof bowl. Blow balloons up into three different sizes; tie ends. Spray balloons lightly with oil. Working with one balloon at a time, hold the balloon upside down over the bowl of chocolate. Spoon chocolate over the balloon, from about halfway down, making sure it covers the rounded top. Gently shake excess chocolate from balloon. Sprinkle confetti over chocolate on two balloons, and use a clothes peg to hang balloons until set (this keeps the balloons from resting on the chocolate and flattening it whilst drying). Once set, carefully pierce a hole in each balloon; allow to deflate. Remove the balloon from inside the chocolate shells.

2 Meanwhile, tint frosting blue. Secure one cake to cake board with a little frosting. Spread cake top with a little frosting; top with remaining cake. Spread top and side of cake with remaining frosting; swirling top to resemble clouds.

3 Re-melt chocolate if necessary. Cut one sour strap into thin lengths. Using picture as a guide, drape around balloon, securing with a little melted chocolate; decorate with confetti, using a little melted chocolate to secure.

4 Dip blunt ends of skewers into melted chocolate. Push skewers, pointy-ends down, into the cake, pushing right down to the base. Before the chocolate sets, carefully position balloons onto skewers.

5 Cut wafers into 12 x 2cm (¾-inch) squares; stick upright into the frosting to create balloon baskets.

6 Cut remaining sour straps into 5mm (¼-inch) wide strips. Drape around side of cake and push into frosting to secure. Using picture as a guide, position mints on cake; secure with a little extra frosting, if necessary.

TIP Remove the skewers before serving the cake.

NUMBERS

TIP *Remove small lollies and decorations from cake before serving to babies and infants, as these can be a choking hazard.*

YOU'RE NUMBER ONE, BABY!

TAKES UNDER 1 HOUR

EQUIPMENT

28cm x 33cm (11¼-inch x 13¼-inch) rectangular cake board (page 112)

CAKE

375g (12 ounces) white chocolate Melts

3 x 250g (8-ounce) packets Tina Wafers (24 strawberry, 24 vanilla, 12 chocolate)

DECORATIONS

1 strawberry sour strap

4 sugar-coated pink marshmallows

3 party ring biscuits (1 pink, 1 purple, 1 white)

6 raspberry lollies

4 pink Smarties

2 purple Smarties

8 pink popped popcorn kernels

3 purple popped popcorn kernels

1 Cut thin strips from the strawberry strap. Roll tightly and place under a heavy object for at least 20 minutes, or until ready to decorate, to curl the strap.

2 Melt chocolate (page 113). Position 12 strawberry wafers in a '1' shape on the cake board using a little white chocolate to secure to the board. Cut one wafer in half diagonally for the top of the '1'; using picture as a guide, position halved wafer at top of number. Spread 2 tablespoons chocolate over strawberry wafers; top with a layer of vanilla wafers, cutting one wafer in half diagonally. Repeat with chocolate wafers, remaining vanilla wafers, then strawberry wafers.

3 Drizzle remaining chocolate over wafers. Top with remaining lollies, biscuits and popcorn.

TIP *Remove small lollies and decorations from cake before serving to babies and infants, as these can be a choking hazard.*

TERRIFIC TWOS

TAKES UP TO 1 HOUR (+ STANDING)

EQUIPMENT

number 2 template (page 115)

30cm x 40cm (12-inch x 16-inch) rectangular cake board (page 112)

CAKE

1½ x 453g (14½-ounce) tubs vanilla frosting

yellow and red food colouring

1 x 450g (14½-ounce) packaged double unfilled sponge cake slabs

DECORATIONS

4 chocolate cream-filled biscuits

1 brown Smartie

1 large white marshmallow

1 mini white marshmallow

7cm (2¾-inch) piece licorice strap, cut into a thin strip

1 Tint frosting yellow. Secure long sides of cakes together using a little frosting. Using a small sharp knife, cut cake using template. Using picture as a guide, secure cakes together on the cake board with a little frosting to form the number 2.

2 Reserve ½ cup of frosting in a microwave-safe bowl. Use a fork to spread remaining frosting all over cake.

3 Twist biscuits in half. Leave one half only with filling; remove and discard filling from remaining biscuits.

4 Press Smartie into biscuit with filling to make eye; place on cake. Cut marshmallow and mini marshmallow in half diagonally; trim into triangular shapes to form 'fangs'. Using picture as a guide, arrange licorice strap and fangs to make mouth.

5 Tint reserved frosting with a little red colouring to make bright orange. Microwave for 20 seconds on HIGH (100%) or until melted. Arrange remaining biscuits on a wire rack over an oven tray. Pour frosting over biscuits; stand for 1 hour or until set enough to handle. Place on cake, trimming a few for the edges.

IT'S A PIRATE'S LIFE FOR ME

TAKES UP TO 1 HOUR

EQUIPMENT

6.5cm (2¾-inch) round cutter

30cm x 40cm (12-inch x 16-inch) rectangular cake board (page 112)

CAKE

1 x 460g (14½-ounce) packaged double unfilled sponge cake rounds

1½ x 453g (14½-ounce) tubs vanilla frosting

DECORATIONS

160g (5-ounce) packet extreme red sour strap

7 white round mints

40cm (16-inch) piece black licorice strap

blue food colouring

2 milk arrowroot biscuits, crushed coarsely

1 mini wafer stick

3 spearmint leaves

1 square chocolate-coated honeycomb

1 tablespoon gold soft sugar pearls

1 Level cake tops, if necessary; turn cakes cut-side down. Use the cutter to cut through the centre of each cake. Using the picture as a guide, trim the cake 'rings' to form the number 3; secure to cake board with a little frosting.

2 Reserve ½ cup of frosting. Spread remaining frosting over top and sides of cake.

3 Using the picture as a guide, trim the edges of the red sour strap to fit the cake as a stripy shirt and head scarf; position on cake. Decorate head scarf with mints, securing with a little frosting. Trim the black licorice strap to make an eye patch and moustache; secure on cake.

4 Marble reserved frosting with blue colouring; spread over base of cake for waves. Sprinkle with biscuit crumbs for sand. Position wafer stick for palm tree trunk. Cut spearmint leaves in half and position on tree for palm leaves. Use a knife to cut the top off honeycomb for the treasure chest, top with sugar pearls.

TIP *Remove small lollies and decorations from cake before serving to babies and infants, as these can be a choking hazard.*

ROAD WORK CREW

TAKES UP TO 1 HOUR

EQUIPMENT

30cm x 40cm (12-inch x 16-inch) rectangular cake board (page 112)

CAKE

1 x 450g (14½-ounce) packaged double unfilled sponge cake slabs

3 x 453g (14½-ounce) tubs vanilla frosting

black, yellow and orange food colouring

DECORATIONS

1 curled licorice strap

black writing icing

2 silver cachous

6 white Tic Tacs

3 plain chocolate cookies

2 pieces chocolate-coated honeycomb

6 spearmint leaves, halved, trimmed into pointy bushes

2 tablespoons round green sprinkles

1 each red, orange and green fruit rings

chocolate malt stick biscuits, optional

1   Cut sponge slabs in half lengthways. Using picture as a guide, trim the cake to form the number 4. Secure cake pieces together on the cake board with a little frosting. Tint ⅓ cup of frosting grey using the black colouring, then divide remaining frosting into 2 medium bowls; tint one yellow and one orange.

2   Spread orange frosting on sides of cake; spread yellow frosting on top of cake.

3   Use the curled centre part of the licorice strap to make a wheel – cut the still-curled strap in half horizontally to make 2 thinner wheels. Using the picture as a guide, use the grey frosting and writing icing to make the hub caps; place a silver cachous in the centre.

4   Spread remaining grey frosting over top of cake to make the road; arrange Tic Tacs down the centre to make the road lines.

5   Crush chocolate cookies finely to make soil; break up honeycomb for rocks. Using picture as a guide, position soil, rocks, wheels, remaining lollies, biscuits and toy truck on and around cake.

TIP *You will need a small toy truck, and other construction toys, if you like, to decorate.*

TIPS *We used mini cupcakes with a 4.5cm/1¾-inch diameter top. Make sure you remove the toothpicks from Lochnessie's head before serving.*

LOCHNESSIE

TAKES OVER 1 HOUR (+ STANDING)

EQUIPMENT

25cm x 40cm (10-inch x 16-inch) rectangular cake board (page 112)

2 toothpicks

CAKE

11 mini cupcakes, uniced

1 x 453g (14½-ounce) tub vanilla frosting

blue and green food colouring

DECORATIONS

4 rice cookie rings

1 sugar-coated doughnut

2 tablespoons rainbow choc-chips

1 white mini marshmallow

1 apple licorice

2 small white meringues, crushed

1 Remove any icing from cupcakes, if necessary. Tint two-thirds of the frosting pale blue. Spread some of the frosting onto cupcakes; tint any leftover pale blue frosting a darker blue. Swirl the darker frosting through the lighter frosting. Arrange cakes on cake board in the shape of a number 5; secure to board with a little frosting.

2 Cut rice cookies in half. Cut doughnut into quarters; reserve one doughnut quarter for head, discard remaining doughnut quarters.

3 Tint remaining frosting green in a microwave-safe bowl. Microwave on HIGH (100%) for 20 seconds or until melted. Dip biscuits and Lochnessie's head into green frosting to coat; allow excess to drip off. Place onto baking paper. Press a few rainbow choc-chips onto each rice biscuit half and onto head. Keep Lochnessie's head upright with toothpicks; stand at room temperature for 1 hour or until set.

4 Cut marshmallow in half. Secure a purple choc-chip onto each marshmallow with a little frosting. Using picture as a guide, press onto either side of head for eyes.

5 Using picture as a guide, arrange biscuits to create Lochnessie's humps. Secure head to first cupcake with toothpicks. Cut licorice into a point and insert into last cupcake for tail. Sprinkle meringue around Lochnessie's humps for foaming water.

DRAGONFIRE

TAKES OVER 1 HOUR (+ STANDING)

EQUIPMENT

number six template (page 115)

30cm x 40cm (12-inch x 16-inch) round cake board (page 112)

baking paper

rolling pin

CAKE

1½ x 453g (14½-ounce) tubs vanilla frosting

green, yellow and blue food colouring

1 x 450g (14½-ounce) packaged double unfilled sponge cake slabs

DECORATIONS

5 ice-cream wafers

10 yellow boiled lollies

10 orange boiled lollies

10 red boiled lollies

1 brown M&M

1 large white round mint

11 green Smarties

16 green M&M's

50 green mini M&M's

3 yellow jelly beans, halved crossways

4 green jelly beans, halved crossways

1 Tint half the frosting green. Divide remaining frosting into two microwave-safe bowls; tint one yellow and the other blue. Secure long sides of cakes together using a little green frosting. Using a small sharp knife, cut cake using template. Using picture as a guide, secure cakes together on the cake board with a little frosting to form the number 6. Cover top and sides of cake with green frosting.

2 Cut 1 wafer diagonally into a triangle. Cut the remaining 4 wafers into 4 smaller triangles. Place triangles on a wire rack over a sheet of baking paper. Microwave blue frosting on HIGH (100%) for 20 seconds or until melted. Pour over small triangles. Repeat with yellow frosting and pour over large triangle. Stand at room temperature for 1 hour or until set.

3 Meanwhile, place boiled lollies, in separate colours, on baking paper-lined microwave-safe plates. Microwave, one colour at a time, on HIGH (100%) for 45 seconds or until melted. Without touching the melted lolly, pour immediately onto a sheet of baking paper; top with another sheet of baking paper. Using a rolling pin, roll to spread thinly. Stand until set. Repeat with remaining boiled lollies.

4 Secure brown M&M to the mint with a little frosting; position on dragon for eye. Using picture as a guide, decorate cake with remaining lollies.

5 Break boiled lollies into shards. Place on cake board near mouth for fire. Using picture as a guide, insert blue wafer spikes around edge of cake; position yellow triangle on top of cake for wing.

MISCHIEVOUS MONKEYS

TAKES UNDER 1 HOUR

EQUIPMENT

35cm x 45cm (14-inch x 18-inch) rectangular cake board (page 112)

1 small disposable piping bag

CAKE

2 x 400g (12½-ounce) packaged jam sponge rolls

1 x 453g (14½-ounce) tub chocolate frosting

2 tablespoons cocoa powder

DECORATIONS

2 rainbow sour straps

50g (1½ ounces) milk chocolate Melts, plus 9 extra

3 chocolate cream-filled biscuits, halved, filling removed

6 white choc-chips

17 banana lollies

10cm (4-inch) piece black licorice strap

1 Using picture as a guide, arrange sponge rolls on the cake board, trimming to form a number '7' shape. Secure to cake board with a little frosting.

2 Spread frosting over top and sides of cake. Sift cocoa powder over cake. Using a small knife or skewer, mark lines in frosting to form tree rounds.

3 Trim green part from sour straps into thin strips (you only need the green part for this cake).

4 Melt the 50g chocolate (page 113). Place melted chocolate in the piping bag; snip a small hole at the end. Using a little chocolate, attach 3 of the extra chocolate Melts to 3 biscuit halves to form monkeys' faces. Attach 2 choc-chips to each biscuit to form eyes, and 2 chocolate Melts to the back of biscuits to form ears. Pipe monkeys' pupils, nostrils and mouth with the melted chocolate.

5 Arrange bananas on cake in bunches; twist green sour strap to form vines. Arrange monkeys' heads on and around cake; place remaining biscuit halves underneath and beside heads to form bodies. Cut licorice strap into thin strips; position on monkeys to form the arms.

GIANT DOUGHNUTS

TAKES UNDER 1 HOUR

EQUIPMENT

5cm (2-inch) round cutter

20cm x 40cm (8-inch x 16-inch) rectangular cake board (page 112)

CAKE

1 x 460g (14½-ounce) packaged double unfilled sponge cake rounds

2½ x 453 (14½-ounce) tubs vanilla frosting

¼ x 453 (14½-ounce) tub chocolate frosting

pink and blue food colouring

DECORATIONS

pastel sprinkles

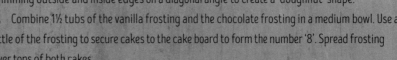

1   Use the round cutter to remove centre of each cake. Round the top of the cakes' edges by trimming outside and inside edges on a diagonal angle to create a 'doughnut' shape.

2   Combine 1½ tubs of the vanilla frosting and the chocolate frosting in a medium bowl. Use a little of the frosting to secure cakes to the cake board to form the number '8'. Spread frosting over tops of both cakes.

3   Evenly divide remaining vanilla frosting between 2 small microwave-safe bowls; colour one pink and one blue. Microwave, separately, on HIGH (100%) for 20 seconds or until melted. Using picture as a guide, pour blue frosting over one of the cakes; drizzle with a little of the pink frosting. Pour remaining pink frosting over remaining cake; sprinkle with pastel sprinkles.

MERMAID PRINCESS

TAKES OVER 1 HOUR (+ STANDING)

EQUIPMENT

number nine template (page 115)

30cm x 40cm (12-inch x 16-inch) rectangular cake board (page 112)

CAKE

1 x 453g (14½-ounce) tub vanilla frosting

pink food colouring

1 x 450g (14½-ounce) packaged double unfilled sponge cake slabs

DECORATIONS

3 x 240g (7½-ounce) packets soft fruit salad jellies

50g (1½ ounces) white chocolate Melts

3 ice-cream wafers

2 teaspoons pink sugar sprinkles

3 silver cachous

4 white mini marshmallows, cut in half crossways

1 Tint frosting pale pink. Secure cakes, long sides together, using a little frosting. Using a small sharp knife, cut cake using template. Using picture as a guide, secure cakes together on the cake board with a little frosting to form the number '9'. Spread cake with remaining frosting.

2 Using a sharp knife, cut jellies in half lengthways. Using picture as a guide, layer jellies, cut-side up, over top of cake for scales.

3 Melt chocolate (page 113). Using picture as a guide, trim corners from 2 wafers to make mermaid's tail. Spread each piece with chocolate; place on a wire rack. Sprinkle with sugar sprinkles, more generously at top end; stand at room temperature until set.

4 Using picture as a guide, trim remaining wafer into a crown. Attach cachous and marshmallow to crown with a little melted chocolate. Position tail and crown on cake.

LIFE ON THE FARM

TAKES UP TO 1 HOUR

EQUIPMENT

6cm (2½-inch) round cutter

32cm (12¾-inch) square cake board (page 112)

CAKE

1 x 400g (12½-ounce) packaged madeira cake

1 x 460g (14½-ounce) packaged double unfilled sponge cake rounds

1 x 453g (14½-ounce) tub vanilla frosting

green food colouring

DECORATIONS

7 pretzel sticks

4 butternut snap biscuits

6 chocolate ripple biscuits

200g (6½ ounces) blue Smarties

9 orange mini runt fruits

3 red berry runt fruits

¼ cup green nerds

3 white mini marshmallows

3 mini black jubes (mixed berry jols)

2 spearmint leaves

¼ cup yellow Smarties

1 small toy dump truck

1 Trim top of madeira cake to same height as the sponge cake. Cut a 6cm (2½-inch) hole from centre of one cake round (you only need one cake round for this recipe; discard or keep the remaining cake round for another use). Secure cakes to cake board with a little frosting.

2 Tint frosting green. Spread frosting over tops and sides of cakes. Using picture as a guide, place pretzel sticks on cakes for fences, trimming to fit each 'paddock'.

3 Blend or process butternut biscuits until coarsely crushed. Blend or process chocolate biscuits until finely crushed. Using picture as a guide, sprinkle crushed butternut biscuits over 2 paddocks and crushed chocolate biscuits over 3 paddocks. Drag a fork through the frosting on the remaining green paddocks. Spoon blue Smarties into the centre of the round cake to make a dam.

4 Using picture as a guide, arrange runts and nerds on paddocks.

5 Use marshmallows for sheep bodies; attach jubes onto marshmallow for heads, securing with a little frosting if necessary. Place sheep into paddock. Place spearmint leaves on cake for trees. Fill dump truck with yellow Smarties and position near cake.

FANTASY & FAIRIES

DESERTED ISLAND

TAKES UP TO 1 HOUR (+ REFRIGERATION)

EQUIPMENT

3-litre (12-cup) straight-sided round clear glass bowl

4cm (1½-inch) round fluted cutter

3 thick wooden skewers, about 25cm (10 inches) long

DECORATIONS

4 x 85g (3-ounce) packets blueberry jelly crystals

4 tablespoons gelatine powder

8 small strawberries, hulled

½ rockmelon (1kg)

½ pineapple (750g), peeled (see tip)

½ honeydew melon (1kg), peeled (see tip)

1 Prepare half the jelly according to packet instructions, adding half the gelatine to the jelly crystals. Strain into the clear glass bowl. Refrigerate for 2 hours or until almost set.

2 Cut strawberries in half lengthways. Cut a triangle shape into the pointy end of half the strawberries. Using picture as a guide, press strawberry halves onto the inside surface of the bowl, just above the jelly line, then press remaining triangular strawberry pieces for fish tails.

3 Prepare remaining jelly according to packet instructions, adding remaining gelatine to the jelly crystals. Cool to room temperature. Gently pour enough of the jelly into bowl until it comes about a third of the way up the fish. Refrigerate for 1 hour or until almost set, then pour the remaining jelly into the bowl and refrigerate for 2 hours or until set.

4 Cut rockmelon into 5mm (¼-inch) thick slices. Using the fluted cutter, cut rounds from rockmelon slices (you need about 22 rounds).

5 Hold skewers together and push pointy ends into rounded top of pineapple; remove skewers, then reinsert skewers, blunt-side down, pushing firmly into the pineapple. Using picture as a guide, thread rockmelon onto skewers to make tree trunk, stopping 3cm (1¼-inches) from top.

6 Cut thin and irregular zig-zag shapes around edges of honeydew melon for palm tree canopy. Place honeydew canopy on top of tree trunk, pressing gently into skewers to secure.

7 Place island and tree on top of jelly; refrigerate until ready to serve.

TIP You may need to buy a whole pineapple and honeydew melon and cut crossways in half; when peeling, keep the shape rounded at one end (see picture, right).

TIP If you don't have a clear glass bowl, set the jelly in a ring pan, adding 2 teaspoons extra dissolved gelatine powder, then turn it onto a serving platter.

RAINBOW CAKE

TAKES UP TO 1 HOUR

EQUIPMENT

30cm (12-inch) round cake board (page 112)

CAKE

1½ x 453g (14½-ounce) tubs vanilla frosting

blue gel food colouring

2 x 460g (14½-ounce) packaged double unfilled sponge cake rounds

DECORATIONS

rainbow star confetti/sprinkles

1 rainbow sour strap

3 white tangfastic marshmallows, halved

1 white marshmallow, halved

8 mini white marshmallows, halved

1 Tint frosting blue. Sandwich three cakes together using a little frosting (discard or keep the remaining cake round for another use), then secure cake to cake board with a little more frosting. Spread remaining frosting over top and side of cake. Push rainbow confetti onto side of cake.

2 Using picture as a guide, push each end of sour strap into frosting. Arrange marshmallows on either side of rainbow in cloud clusters.

HIPPIE VAN

TAKES OVER 1 HOUR

EQUIPMENT

30cm x 40cm (12-inch x 16-inch) rectangular cake board (page 112)

CAKE

1 x 450g (14½-ounce) packaged double unfilled sponge cake slabs

2 x 453g (14½-ounce) tubs vanilla frosting

green food colouring

DECORATIONS

50g (1½ ounces) white chocolate Melts

50g (1½ ounces) 100s and 1000s sprinkles

10cm (4-inch) piece black licorice strap

2 rainbow sour straps

3 pretzel sticks

6 extreme red sour straps

3 each red, purple and yellow oval jubes

4 chocolate cream-filled biscuits

14 edible cake decorating flowers

2 x 100s and 1000s coated white chocolate buttons

2 yellow skittles

1 Trim and stack cakes to form a 20cm long x 9cm wide x 7cm high rectangle (8-inch x 3¾-inch x 2¾-inch). Use a little frosting to secure cake pieces together; secure cake to cake board with a little frosting. Tint half the remaining frosting light green. Using picture as a guide, cover the bottom half of the cake with green frosting and the top half with white frosting, making a 'V' shape at the front of the van.

2 Melt chocolate (page 113). Draw a surfboard shape on a piece of baking paper, turn paper over. Use a spoon to thickly pour and carefully spread chocolate over the surfboard drawing. Leave until almost set, then trim shape neatly; leave until set, remove paper. Spread a little more chocolate (re-melt if necessary) on sides of surfboard; press 100s and 1000s into chocolate. Using picture as a guide, cut some of the licorice strap into a strip and circle to make a leg rope for the surfboard; attach with melted chocolate.

3 Cut the edge of one rainbow strap into a scallop shape. Spread melted chocolate on opposite straight edge of strap. Secure both rainbow straps together at a 90° angle to make awning for the van; stand until set. Cut pretzel sticks in half and push 6 pieces into one side of the van to make a shelf for the awning to rest on.

4 Cut sour straps into 2 heart shapes; cut remaining strap into thin strips. Use the strips to outline van and awning.

5 Using picture as a guide, cut the licorice strap into strips to make the 'peace' sign; secure to van with a little melted chocolate. Cut jubes lengthways into quarters to make flowers; secure flowers and hearts to van. Cut leftover pieces of yellow jube into small rounds; position on centre of jube 'flowers'.

6 Using the picture as a guide, decorate van with remaining decorations.

BALLERINA

TAKES UP TO 1 HOUR (+ FREEZING & REFRIGERATION)

Melt 300g (9½ ounces) white chocolate Melts (page 113). Halve 6 mini jam rolls crossways. Dip 12 thick wooden skewers into chocolate; insert a skewer into the base of each jam roll. Place on an oven tray; freeze for 10 minutes or until chocolate has set. Dip rolls in remaining chocolate (re-melt if necessary) one at a time. Sprinkle pops with ½ cup pink decorating sugar to coat. Stand upright in an egg carton or styrofoam block in the fridge until set. Gently scrunch 60 large pink cupcake cases together (scrunch 5 at a time); cut a small hole into centres. Push 5 cases onto each skewer to form tutu.

FAIRY POP

TAKES UP TO 1 HOUR (+ FREEZING & REFRIGERATION)

Melt 300g (9½ ounces) white chocolate Melts (page 113). Halve 6 mini jam rolls crossways. Dip 12 thick wooden skewers into chocolate; insert a skewer into the base of each jam roll. Place on an oven tray; freeze for 10 minutes or until chocolate has set. Dip rolls in remaining chocolate (re-melt if necessary) one at a time. Sprinkle pops with ½ cup green sprinkles. Stand upright in an egg carton or styrofoam block in the fridge until set. Cut 24 pink sugar coated marshmallows in half. Attach 4 halves to the back of each pop with a little extra melted chocolate. Using picture as a guide, trim 12 green cupcake cases in a zig-zag shape. Stack each on top of 2 pink patterned cupcake cases. Make a cut in centre of paper cases and insert onto skewers to form skirt.

CHEAT'S CAKE POPS

EACH RECIPE DECORATES 12 POPS

HULA GIRL

TAKES UP TO 1 HOUR (+ FREEZING & REFRIGERATION)

Melt 300g (9½ ounces) white chocolate Melts (page 113). Halve 6 mini jam rolls crossways. Dip 12 thick wooden skewers into chocolate; insert a skewer into the base of each jam roll. Place on an oven tray; freeze for 10 minutes or until chocolate has set. Dip rolls in remaining chocolate (re-melt if necessary) one at a time. Secure 12 halved Maltesers onto pops to form coconut bra; attach about 14 mini fondant flowers to base of each pop. Stand upright in an egg carton or styrofoam block in the fridge until set. Using picture as a guide, cut 36 large cupcake case edges into strips (cut 3 at a time). Make a cut in centre of paper cases and insert three each onto skewers to form skirt.

POP PRINCESS

TAKES UP TO 1 HOUR (+ FREEZING & REFRIGERATION)

Melt 300g (9½ ounces) white chocolate Melts (page 113). Halve 6 mini jam rolls crossways. Dip 12 thick wooden skewers into chocolate; insert a skewer into the base of each jam roll. Place on an oven tray; freeze for 10 minutes or until chocolate has set. Dip rolls in remaining chocolate (re-melt if necessary) one at a time. Stand upright in an egg carton or styrofoam block in the fridge until set. Slice 30 square purple jubes into 4 slices; press purple choc-chips into centre of each jube. Using a little melted chocolate, attach jubes to base of pops. Cut a scallop edge around 24 large cupcake cases. Make a cut in centre of paper cases and insert 2 scalloped and 1 plain paper case onto each skewer to form skirt.

THE MARSHMAHAL

TAKES UP TO 1 HOUR

EQUIPMENT

**30cm (12-inch) round cake board
(page 112)**

CAKE

**2 x 453g (14½-ounce) tubs vanilla
frosting**

pink food colouring

**1 x 460g (14½-ounce) packaged
double unfilled sponge cake rounds**

DECORATIONS

8 flat-based ice-cream cones

4 mini choc-chip muffins, uniced

1 large choc-chip muffin , uniced

2 large pink muffin paper cases

1 long marshmallow twist rope

1 yellow meringue twirl

5 pink musk sticks

**20 coloured peaked Haribo
marshmallows**

**10 mini pink and white meringue
kisses**

small bow and 4 flag cake toppers

1 Tint frosting pink. Secure one cake to cake board with a little frosting. Spread top of cake with a thin layer of frosting, top with remaining cake. Reserve 1½ cups of the frosting. Cover top and side of cake with remaining frosting.

2 Remove paper cases from mufffins, if necessary. Stack 2 ice-cream cones together securing with a little of the reserved frosting inside each one. Press a mini muffin inside cone then place at one side of cake. Repeat with remaining cones and mini muffins; arrange around cake. Top cake and muffins with large spoonfuls of the reserved frosting.

3 Using picture as a guide, place the large muffin into the paper cases then position muffin on top of cake. Twist marshmallow rope into a spiral and place on top of muffin; place yellow meringue on top, then top with a small bow.

4 Trim musk sticks for door; press onto cake. Position marshmallows and meringue kisses on cake; insert cake topper flags into marshmallows.

EDIBLE NECKLACES

Each recipe makes 1. You will also need a wool needle and thin elastic.

FRUITY NECKLACE

TAKES 10 MINUTES

Using a clean wool needle and new thin elastic as string, thread 9 strawberries, 6 green grapes and 7 mandarin segments onto elastic. Tie end of elastic to secure. Keep refrigerated until just before serving.

MARSHMALLOW PEARL NECKLACE

TAKES 10 MINUTES

Using a clean wool needle and new thin elastic as string, thread 100g (3 ounces) assorted marshmallows onto elastic. Tie end of elastic to secure.

WRAPPED SWEET SURPRISE NECKLACE

TAKES 20 MINUTES

Place a 20cm x 55cm (8-inch x 20-inch) piece of clear cellophane on work bench. Position an assortment of lollies along one long end of cellophane at 2cm (¾-inch) intervals. Roll cellophane to enclose lollies. Secure ends with sticky tape. Tie coloured twine between each lolly to keep lollies separate. Tie ends together to form a necklace.

TROPICAL NECKLACE

TAKES 10 MINUTES

Using a clean wool needle and new thin elastic as string, thread assorted brightly-coloured lollies onto elastic. Tie end of elastic to secure.

MIAMI NIGHTS

TAKES OVER 1 HOUR (+ REFRIGERATION)

EQUIPMENT

30cm (12-inch) square cake board (page 112)

CAKE

½ seedless watermelon (2kg)

2 x 85g (3-ounce) packets creaming soda jelly crystals

4 teaspoons gelatine powder

DECORATIONS

1 sherbet bracelet

2 green jelly rings

2 sherbet lollipops

2 coloured mini paper cases

1 large coloured cupcake paper case

2 cocktail umbrellas

1 rainbow sour strap

1 Trim a little off the base of the watermelon so it sits flat and stable. Using a sharp knife, mark an oval shape on top of the watermelon, 5cm (2-inches) from the edge. Using the oval shape as a guide, hollow out the watermelon until it is 10cm (4-inch) deep, creating steps on one side, if you like. Place on a large tray.

2 Make jelly following packet directions, adding the gelatine to the jelly crystals. Refrigerate for 20 minutes, then pour into the watermelon (pour any extra jelly into small cups to serve at the party). Refrigerate for 5 hours or until jelly has set.

3 Position watermelon on cake board. Carefully snip sherbet bracelet and arrange on top of jelly to form a pool lane marker. Place green jelly rings around pool for lifebuoys. Turn sherbet lollipops upside down; place coloured cases on top to form umbrellas (we covered the large cupcake case with a small cupcake case to make one of the umbrellas). Position all umbrellas around pool edge. Cut rainbow sour strap into 3 lengths for pool towels, place around pool.

TIPS Start this the day before serving to give the jelly time to set. Cut coloured plastic or paper straws to make the pool steps, if you like; secure together with a little sticky tape.

WOODLAND GROTTO

TAKES OVER 1 HOUR

EQUIPMENT

30cm (12-inch) round cake board (page 112)

7 toothpicks

CAKE

1 x 585g (1¼-pound) packaged round chocolate mud cake

1½ x 453g (14½-ounce) tubs chocolate frosting

DECORATIONS

1 large double choc-chip muffin

3 mini choc-chip muffins

½ x 250g (8-ounce) packet chocolate ripple biscuits

½ x 400g (12½-ounce) packet digestive biscuits

green food colouring

7 white mini marshmallows

9 raspberry lollies

50g (1½-ounce) tube each of white and dark chocolate writing icing

3 spearmint leaves

2 choc-vanilla mallow bites

50g (1½ ounces) dark chocolate Melts

2 pfeffernusse spice biscuits (German spice cookies)

1 Remove icing from cake. Level cake top if necessary; turn cake cut-side down. Secure cake to cake board with a little frosting. Spread top and side of cake with a little more frosting. Remove paper cases and icing from muffins, if necessary; spread muffins all over with frosting. Using the picture as a guide, position muffins on top and around cake.

2 Blend or process chocolate ripple biscuits into coarse crumbs. Using the picture as a guide, arrange crushed biscuits on and around cake to resemble soil.

3 Blend or process digestive biscuits into coarse crumbs. Remove ½ cup of the crumbs. Add green colouring to the remaining crumbs, and pulse until crumbs are evenly coloured. Sprinkle crumbs on and around cake to resemble grass.

4 To make mushrooms, thread mini marshmallow onto toothpicks; top with raspberry lollies. Using white writing icing, decorate mushroom tops with spots. Position mushrooms and mushroom tops on cake. Split spearmint leaves in half lengthways; arrange on cakes in clusters. Position mallow bites on larger cake for rocks.

5 Melt chocolate (page 113). Dip three-quarters of each spice biscuit into melted chocolate, press reserved plain crumbs onto chocolate. Use dark writing icing to draw eyes and nose on hedgehogs; place on and around cake.

TIP *Make sure you remove the toothpicks before serving.*

CREATURES & CRITTERS

TIP *We used red gel colouring for this recipe to get an intense colour. If using a liquid colour you may need to add some sifted icing (confectioners') sugar to stop the frosting from splitting.*

PINCHY THE CRAB

TAKES UNDER 1 HOUR (+ STANDING)

EQUIPMENT

32cm (12¾-inch) round cake board (page 112)

CAKE

1 x 460g (14½-ounce) packaged double unfilled sponge cake rounds

1 x 453g (14½-ounce) tub vanilla frosting

red gel food colouring

DECORATIONS

2 fortune cookies

14 raspberry licorice pieces

2 blue round lollipops

2 pfeffernusse spice biscuits (German spice cookies), or large white round mints or marshmallows

2 brown M&M's

2 tablespoons red M&M's

2 tablespoons red mini M&M's

1 Secure one cake to cake board with a little frosting (you only need one cake round for this recipe; discard or keep the remaining cake round for another use). Tint remaining frosting red. Reserve 1½ cups of the frosting in a microwave-safe bowl. Spread remaining frosting over top and side of cake.

2 Microwave reserved frosting on HIGH (100%) for 20 seconds or until melted. Dip fortune cookies into frosting to coat. Place cookies on a wire rack over baking paper. Stand for 1 hour or until set.

3 Using picture as a guide, position licorice pieces around cake for legs. Position fortune cookies for claws.

4 Push lollipops into side of cake for eyes. Slide a spice biscuit underneath each eye. Secure brown M&M's to eyes with a little frosting. Top cake with red M&M's.

NEST EGG

TAKES OVER 1 HOUR (+ STANDING)

EQUIPMENT

10cm (4-inch) round cutter

**30cm (12-inch) round cake board
(page 112)**

CAKE

**1 x 460g (14½-ounce) packaged
double unfilled sponge cake rounds**

DECORATIONS

**225g (7 ounces) milk chocolate
Melts**

**2 tablespoons crunchy peanut
butter**

**2 x 100g (3-ounce) packets
fried noodles**

**3 x 7cm (2¾-inch) long chocolate
Easter eggs**

1 Using the round cutter, cut a hollow from the centre of one cake, without cutting all the way through to the base; discard centre cake piece. (You only need one cake round for this recipe; discard or keep the remaining cake round for another use.) Secure cake to cake board.

2 Place chocolate and peanut butter in a large microwave-safe bowl. Microwave on HIGH (100%), in 30-second bursts, stirring, until melted and smooth. Add noodles to chocolate mixture; stir until noodles are well-coated.

3 Press noodle mixture evenly around base and side of cake. Stand at room temperature for 1 hour or until set.

4 Fill nest with chocolate eggs. Slice cake with a hot knife to serve.

HELLO MISS KITTY

TAKES OVER 1 HOUR (+ STANDING)

EQUIPMENT

**30cm (12-inch) round cake board
(page 112)**

CAKE

**1½ x 453g (14½-ounce) tubs
vanilla frosting**

purple and pink food colouring

**2 x 460g (14½-ounce) packaged
double unfilled sponge cake rounds**

DECORATIONS

**25g (¾ ounce) white chocolate
Melts, plus 2 extra**

**8cm (3¼ inches) licorice bootlace,
cut into 4 equal pieces**

2 ice-cream wafers

1 waffle ice-cream cone

2 brown Smarties

1 round pink fizzo ball

large pink bow tie

15 white mini marshmallows

1 Tint one tub of frosting purple. Stack three cakes together with a little frosting between each layer (discard or keep the remaining cake round for another use). Secure to cake board with a little frosting.

2 Melt the 25g of chocolate (page 113). Secure licorice to extra Melts with a little chocolate for whiskers; stand until set.

3 Cut ice-cream wafers into 2 large triangles for ears and 2 slightly smaller triangles for inner ears. Place remaining ½ tub of frosting in a microwave-safe bowl; tint frosting pink. Microwave on HIGH (100%) for 20 seconds or until melted. Place ice-cream cone and small wafer triangles on a wire rack over a sheet of baking paper; pour over pink frosting to cover. Stand at room temperature for 1 hour or until set.

4 Insert larger triangles on top of cake for ears. Spread purple frosting over top and side of cake and ears; use a fork to roughen surface of frosting for fur.

5 Using the picture as a guide, press Smarties, whiskers and fizzo ball onto cake to make kitty's face. Position bow tie, cone party hat and pink triangles for inner ears. Squash marshmallows; secure around base and on top of party hat.

HOOT HOOT HOORAY

TAKES UP TO 1 HOUR

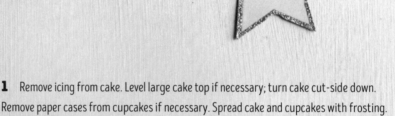

EQUIPMENT

30cm x 40cm (12-inch x 16-inch) rectangular cake board (page 112)

CAKE

1 x 600g (1¼-pound) packaged round chocolate mud cake

4 x 60g (2-ounce) chocolate cupcakes or muffins, uniced

1 x 453g (14½-ounce) tub chocolate frosting

DECORATIONS

2 tablespoons cocoa powder

8 mini chocolate cream-filled biscuits

8 brown mini M&M's

28 orange mini M&M's

2 chocolate cream-filled biscuits

2 brown M&M's

7 orange M&M's

1 large wagon wheel

1 Remove icing from cake. Level large cake top if necessary; turn cake cut-side down. Remove paper cases from cupcakes if necessary. Spread cake and cupcakes with frosting. Dust with sifted cocoa.

2 Carefully twist mini biscuits apart. Cut the uniced halves into two; position in cupcakes for wings. Push brown mini M&M's into iced biscuit halves for eyes; position on cupcakes.

3 Using picture as a guide, position 6 mini orange M&M's on each small owl as talons, and 1 mini orange M&M as a nose.

4 Repeat with larger biscuit (but discard the uniced pieces of biscuits), brown M&M's and orange M&M's for large owl. Cut wagon wheel in half and push into sides of large owl for wings.

FEARLESS LION

TAKES UP TO 1 HOUR

Use a 453g (14½-ounce) tub vanilla frosting to spread over tops of 8 cupcakes; cover with coarsely crushed milk arrowroot biscuits. Insert 2 x 110g (3½-ounce) packets of natural sliced almonds around the cupcakes for the lion's mane. Cut a 25cm (10-inch) piece of black licorice strap into thin strips; cut each strip into 2.5cm (1-inch) pieces. Use black writing icing to stick licorice and a black Jelly Belly jelly bean onto cupcakes to make lion's nose and mouth. Use black writing icing to attach 2 edible white confetti to each face for eyes; squeeze a drop of icing on the confetti for lion's pupils.

PERPLEXED PANDA

TAKES UP TO 1 HOUR

Place 3 cups desiccated coconut in a medium bowl. Spread a 453g (14½-ounce) tub vanilla frosting over the tops of 8 cupcakes; press tops into coconut to cover well. Using picture as a guide, press 5 chocolate chips onto each cupcake to form the ears, eyes and nose. Press a brown candy-coated chocolate chip (from a tub of rainbow choc-chips) onto each cupcake for the mouth. Use black writing icing to stick 2 edible white confetti on each face for eyes; squeeze a drop of icing on confetti for panda's pupils.

CRAZY ANIMAL CRITTERS

YOUCAN TOUCAN

TAKES UP TO 1 HOUR

Reserve 2 tablespoons frosting from 2 x 453g (14½-ounce) tubs vanilla frosting. Tint reserved frosting orange. Tint half the remaining frosting black. Using picture as a guide, spread black frosting in a quarter-moon shape around each cupcake; spread white frosting on the remaining cupcake tops. Using picture as a guide, cut 8 extra thick ice-cream wafers to make beaks. Use a new clean paint brush to paint a little orange frosting on the tips of the top beaks. Attach beaks to cupcakes. Split 4 green jube rings in half; place on centre of cupcakes. Use black writing icing to stick a yellow M&M and an edible white confetti onto jube for eyes; squeeze a drop of icing on confetti for pupils. Cut 1 red sour strap into thin strips; trim strips to fit around front half of the jube rings.

CRAZY CROCODILE

TAKES UP TO 1 HOUR (+ STANDING)

Tint a 453g (14½-ounce) tub vanilla frosting blue; spread over tops of 8 cupcakes. Using the back of a teaspoon, make peaks and waves on frosting. Using picture as a guide, trim 16 pieces of extra thick ice-cream wafers into 9cm x 4.5cm (3¾-inch x 1¾-inch) rectangles, tapering slightly at one short end. Tint a 453g (14½-ounce) tub vanilla frosting green in a microwave-safe bowl. Microwave frosting on HIGH (100%) in 20-second bursts until melted. Dip wafers, one at a time, into green frosting; place on a wire rack over baking paper. On half of the wafers, press 2 large green M&M's for eyes and 2 mini green M&M's for the nose. Stand until set. Use black writing icing to stick 2 edible white confetti to large M&M's; squeeze a drop of icing on confetti for pupils. Place plain green wafers on cupcakes; using a little writing gel, attach 1 white mini marshmallow to the front end of each wafer. Using a little icing, attach the remaining wafer on top to complete the crocodiles' jaws.

Each recipe decorates 8 cupcakes. We used two 320g (10-ounce) packets of uniced cupcakes.

DID YOU KNOW? *A herbivore from the late Cretaceous period, Dravidosaurus stood just 1.2 metres (4 feet) tall and 3 metres (10 feet) long.*

DRAVIDO DINOSAUR

TAKES UP TO 1 HOUR

EQUIPMENT

dinosaur template (page 114)

30cm x 40cm (12-inch x 16-inch) rectangular cake board (page 112)

CAKE

3 x 450g (14½-ounce) packaged double unfilled sponge cake slabs

2 x 453g (14½-ounce) tubs vanilla frosting

green food colouring

DECORATIONS

3 ice-cream wafers

12 green jelly beans

1 green jelly fruit ring

6 orange jelly fruit rings

5 triangle orange jubes

6 oval orange jubes

2 round eclipse mints

2 mini brown M&M's

9 mini white marshmallows

1 Secure 2 cakes, long sides together, with a little frosting. Spread top of cakes with a thin layer of frosting then place 2 cakes on top. Place body, head and tail templates on cake; using a small sharp knife, cut pieces from cake. Stand cake pieces on cake board upright on their long flat edges. Cut 2 of each legs from remaining single cake layer (you only need five cake slabs for this recipe; discard or keep the remaining cake slab for another use).

2 Using the picture as a guide, assemble dinosaur pieces to make body, securing pieces with a little frosting and trimming and shaping pieces to fit; secure cake to cake board with a little frosting. Cut a diamond and 2 triangles from wafers for the spikes; press spikes into top of cake.

3 Tint frosting green; spread all over cake and spikes.

4 Press 3 jelly beans into the front of each leg. Using the picture as a guide, cut fruit rings and jubes in half; press, sugar-side down, into frosting. Press a mint into the centre of each green fruit ring and use a little frosting to attach mini M&M's onto each mint for eyes.

5 Push 2 mini marshmallows into each side at the end of the tail. Cut remaining marshmallows in half diagonally and push into frosting for teeth.

SCIENCE & NATURE

STORM IN A JAR

TAKES OVER 1 HOUR

EQUIPMENT

30cm (12-inch) round cake board (page 112)

30cm (12-inch) wide, 25cm (10-inch) high straight-sided glass bowl

CAKE

2 x 453g (14½-ounce) tubs vanilla frosting

royal blue and black food colouring

1 x 460g (14½-ounce) packaged double unfilled sponge cake rounds

DECORATIONS

1 x 7cm (2¾-inch) long pretzel stick

1 x 7cm (2¾-inch) square waffle

1 piece firm white printer paper

¼ cup blue M&M's

¼ cup blue mini M&M's

¼ cup blue runts

4 meringue kisses, crushed

1   Tint both tubs of frosting blue, one lighter than the other. Add a little black colouring to both to achieve a 'grey blue' storm colour.

2   Secure one cake to cake board with a little frosting. Spread a thin layer of frosting on top of cake and top with remaining cake. Cover top and side of cake with a little of the darker frosting. Using picture as a guide, and with the back of a spoon, pick up and smear both frostings on cake to resemble stormy waves.

3   Press pretzel stick into waffle for boat. Cut paper into an 8cm x 11cm (3¼-inch x 4½-inch) rectangle and a 4cm x 6cm (1½-inch x 2½-inch) rectangle, slightly narrower at one long end. Make small holes in each end and push through the pretzel for sails. Position on cake.

4   Arrange blue lollies on and around cake, sprinkle waves with crushed meringue. Cover cake with the upturned glass bowl.

FROZEN AVALANCHE

TAKES UP TO 1 HOUR (+ FREEZING)

EQUIPMENT

2 large metal oven trays

25cm (10-inch) flat dinner plate or tray with a lip or 25cm (10-inch) round cake board (page 112)

CAKE

8 litres (24 cups) vanilla ice-cream

DECORATIONS

150g (4½ ounces) Ferrero Raffaello coconut cream balls, unwrapped

220g (7 ounce) bottle White Choc Ice Magic

½ cup (40g) desiccated coconut

blue and red cardboard

9 disposable wooden teaspoons

small toy skier

1 Chill metal trays and serving plate in freezer for 30 minutes. Line trays with baking paper. Scoop balls of ice-cream onto chilled trays; freeze for 1 hour.

2 Arrange ice-cream scoops into a pile on the chilled serving plate to create a mountain. Place Raffaello balls in the gaps on the ice-cream mountain.

3 Drizzle mountain with Ice Magic; sprinkle with coconut. Freeze until ready to serve.

4 Meanwhile, cut cardboard into small triangles, secure to spoons with a little glue or sticky tape to make flags.

5 Position flags and skier on cake.

TIP *Remove the toy skier and flags before serving.*

TIP *If you like, decorate with hedgehogs and mushrooms; see page 71 for instructions.*

TREE HOUSE

TAKES OVER 1 HOUR (+ STANDING)

EQUIPMENT

4cm (1½-inch) round cutter

30cm (12-inch) round cake board (page 112)

CAKE

1 x 460g (14½-ounce) packaged double unfilled sponge cake rounds

1 x 453g (14½-ounce) tub vanilla frosting

green food colouring

DECORATIONS

375g (12 ounces) dark chocolate Melts

½ x 205g (6½-ounce) packet chocolate cream-filled biscuits

2 x 23g (¾-ounce) packets mini chocolate cream-filled biscuits

16 ice-cream wafers

4 spearmint leaves, halved lengthways

3 pretzel sticks

¹/₃ x 250g (8-ounce) packet milk arrowroot biscuits

1 rainbow strap, green part only

1 Using the cutter, cut and discard a round from centre of one cake (you only need one cake round for this recipe; discard or keep the remaining cake round for another use). Secure cake to cake board with a little frosting. Tint remaining frosting green. Spread frosting over top and side of cake.

2 Melt chocolate (page 113). Gently twist all chocolate biscuits to separate; discard the cream filling. Stack the larger biscuits 24 biscuits high, securing together with a little melted chocolate. Stack the mini biscuits into small stacks, slightly off-centre, securing with melted chocolate, for branches of tree; stand stacks until set.

3 Spoon 1 tablespoon melted chocolate into the centre hole of cake onto the cake board. Insert the large biscuit stack into the hole, pressing biscuit stack so it sits on the cake board. Stand at room temperature for 1 hour or until set.

4 Place a large sheet of baking paper on work bench. Dip one long edge of a wafer into chocolate; secure to another wafer to create a wafer panel. Repeat 6 times to give a total of 7 wafer panels; leave to set on baking paper.

5 Using the picture as a guide, cut windows and a door into three of the wafer panels. Cut 2 triangles from the remaining unjoined wafers (make the base of the triangle the same length as the short sides of the joined panels). Starting with the floor, dip wafer edges into chocolate and join to make a tree house, making sure each panel is set before attaching another. Use chocolate to secure the roof; stand for 30 minutes or until set.

6 Secure mini biscuit stacks to side of tree house and trunk for branches, holding for at least 1 minute or until the branches are set and secure. Use melted chocolate to attach spearmint leaves onto the branches.

7 Cut 1 pretzel stick into 3 pieces. Dip ends in chocolate and secure between remaining pretzels to make a ladder. Stand until set, then prop against trunk.

8 Blend or process biscuits and food colouring into evenly-coloured crumbs. Sprinkle over base of cake. Cut green section from sour strap into thin strips, twist and curl and position over branches of tree for vines.

TIP Remove toothpicks and toys before serving.

ADVENTURE ISLANDS

TAKES OVER 1 HOUR (+ STANDING)

EQUIPMENT

1 small disposable piping bag

4 toothpicks

50cm (20-inch) square cake board

CAKE

1 choc-chip muffin

4 mini choc-chip muffins

2 x 453g (14½-ounce) tubs vanilla frosting

green oil-based food colouring suitable for chocolate

2 x 460g (14½-ounce) packaged double unfilled sponge cake rounds

DECORATIONS

2 tablespoons blue sanding sugar

1½ x 250g (8-ounce) packets milk arrowroot biscuits

250g (8 ounces) white chocolate Melts

4 pretzel sticks

3 waffle ice-cream cones

2 snack-size Boost bars

8 spearmint leaves

3 choc-vanilla mallow bites

3 chocolate-coated honeycomb and 3 tablespoons gold soft sugar pearls to make treasure chests (see 'It's a Pirate's Life For Me' page 38, for instructions)

small pirate and soldier toys

1 Remove and discard cases from muffins. Spread a little of the frosting over the larger muffin and two of the mini muffins.

2 Cut one cake round crossways into 2 pieces, one piece larger than the other. Using picture as a guide (top island), stack the cut pieces on top of one of the whole cake rounds, smaller piece on top of larger; secure with a little frosting. You should now have a 3-tiered cake and a single-layered cake (you only need three cake rounds for this recipe; discard or keep the remaining cake round for another use).

3 Tint remaining frosting green. Spread green frosting over top and sides of both cakes and remaining mini muffins. Place the green frosted mini muffins on the single-layered cake. Sprinkle blue sanding sugar onto the cake for water.

4 Blend or process biscuits into coarse crumbs. Remove half the crumbs to a medium bowl and set aside. Add green food colouring to remaining crumbs and pulse to colour evenly. Press green biscuit crumbs onto tiered island to coat. Coat plain frosted muffin and mini muffins with some of the plain biscuit crumbs.

5 Melt chocolate (page 113). Place pretzel sticks on a large sheet of baking paper. Reserve ¼ cup of the melted chocolate. Tint remaining chocolate green (page 113). Dip waffle cones into green chocolate to coat, shake off excess; place upside down on the baking paper. Fill piping bag with remaining green chocolate, cut the tip off the bag. Using picture as a guide, pipe a freeform zig-zag pattern on the top half of each pretzel to form a tree; stand 10 minutes or until set. Dip tips of waffle cones into melted white chocolate; allow to set.

6 Insert a toothpick into each end of the Boost bars; push the top one in so only 5mm (¼-inch) is exposed. Leave the bottom one so at least 4cm (1½-inches) is exposed. Push the ends of 4 spearmint leaves together and secure in a cross shape for each tree; push onto top toothpick. Use bottom toothpick to push trees into large muffin.

7 Using picture as a guide, position cakes and muffins onto the cake board; position mallow bites for rocks. Sprinkle remaining plain biscuit crumbs around one of the islands. Place trees, mountains and remaining decorations on cakes and around cake board.

PEARLY SHELLS

TAKES UP TO 1 HOUR (+ STANDING)

EQUIPMENT

30cm x 40cm (12-inch x 16-inch) serving platter

DECORATIONS

1 x 250g (8-ounce) packet milk arrowroot biscuits

100g (3 ounces) white chocolate Melts

6 store-bought pikelets

1 tablespoon dark pink sanding sugar

1 tablespoon pale pink sanding sugar

3 large pearl gum balls

10 pfeffernusse spice biscuits (German spice cookies)

5 pink fizzo balls

4 flat-based ice-cream cones

2 candy bracelets

2 cake topper flags

12 pieces green licorice

2 tablespoons pearl cachous

4 small white meringues

1 Blend or process biscuits into fine crumbs. Sprinkle crumbs over serving platter to cover.

2 Melt chocolate (page 113). Spread melted chocolate over pikelets then sprinkle with sanding sugars. Place a pearl gumball on 3 pikelets; top each with remaining pikelets, on an angle. Secure with melted chocolate; stand until set.

3 Use melted chocolate to join 2 spice biscuits on one edge, flat-sides together. Place a fizzo ball in between biscuits to wedge open. Repeat to make 4 more pearl shells.

4 Stack ice-cream cones together, 2 cones each. Carefully cut candy bracelets open. Use melted chocolate to secure candy beads around ice-cream cones. Insert flag toppers.

5 Cut licorice into thin strips; pinch together into clusters to form seaweed. Arrange in sand along with shells, pearl cachous and meringues.

COMPASS OF DISCOVERY

TAKES UP TO 1 HOUR

EQUIPMENT

30cm (12-inch) round cake board (page 112)

12cm (4¾-inch) and 2.5cm (1-inch) round cutters

CAKE

1 x 453g (14½-ounce) tub vanilla frosting

yellow food colouring

2 x 600g (1¼-pound) packaged white chocolate mud cakes

DECORATIONS

40cm (16-inch) piece black licorice strap

N, S, E & W dark chocolate cake decorating letters

1 extreme red sour strap

1 brown mini M&M

1 rice ring cookie

1 Tint two-thirds of the frosting yellow; reserve ¼ cup of the yellow frosting.

2 Remove icing from cakes. Level cake tops if necessary; turn cakes cut-side down. Secure one cake to the cake board with a little frosting. Cover top and side of cake with yellow frosting. Cut remaining cake in half horizontally then cut one layer into a 12cm round with the cutter (discard or reserve remaining layer and offcuts for another use). Cover top and side of cake with vanilla frosting; using picture as a guide, carefully position onto centre of yellow cake.

3 Trim licorice into 4 triangles 2.5cm high x 1.5cm base (1-inch x ¾-inch), then cut another 4 triangles 5cm high x 1cm base (2-inch x ½-inch). Using picture as a guide, position triangles on centre of cake. Arrange chocolate letters on cake.

4 Cut sour strap into a 2.5cm round with cutter, and a 5cm long thin needle; secure onto cake with a little frosting. Position M&M in centre of direction needle with a little frosting.

5 Spread reserved yellow frosting over ring cookie then push into top edge of cake. Cut remaining licorice into a strip; loop through hole in cookie.

X-RAY MACHINE

TAKES UP TO 1 HOUR

EQUIPMENT

30cm x 40cm (12-inch x 16-inch) rectangular cake board (page 112)

CAKE

2 x 453g (14½-ounce) tubs vanilla frosting

blue and pink food colouring

2 x 450g (14½-ounce) packaged double unfilled sponge cake slabs

DECORATIONS

2 x 1cm (½-inch) thick slices large jam roll

9 white marshmallows

10 white mint discs

3 extra thick ice-cream wafers

2 extreme red sour straps

250g (8-ounce) packet marzipan

6 white round mints

2 yellow gumballs

2 red gumballs

1 green gumball

2 large white marshmallows

1 each red and green fruit rings

1 red Smartie

10cm (4-inch) piece black licorice strap

1   Tint one tub of frosting blue. Tint 2 tablespoons of remaining frosting pink. Secure long sides of 2 cakes together with a little frosting onto cake board. Cover top and sides of cake with blue frosting.

2   Cut another cake slab in half to form 2 rectangles (you only need 3 cake slabs for this recipe; discard or keep remaining cake slab for another use). Place rectangles on right side of blue cake, trimming to fit; cover with some of the vanilla frosting.

3   Cover jam roll slices with vanilla frosting then, using picture as a guide, position on the bottom part of the cake for kidneys. Press marshmallows and mint discs onto cake to form the vertebrae of the spinal column.

4   Carefully trim 2 wafers into large oval shapes and remaining wafer into a heart shape. Spread pink frosting over oval wafers for lungs; place one 'lung' on each side at the top of the spine. Attach the red sour straps onto the heart-shaped wafer; trim to fit shape.

5   Tint half the marzipan dark pink and roll into a 5mm (¼-inch) thick rope. Using the picture as a guide, shape marzipan to look like intestines. Place on cake. Roll remaining marzipan into the same thickness; cut into 6 x 12cm (4¾-inch) and 2 x 24cm (9½-inch) lengths. Position the marzipan pieces on cake to make rib cage. Top with heart.

6   Using the picture as a guide, place round mints on white part of cake for buttons; cut gumballs in half; place on top of each button. Squash large marshmallows and place on cake. Cut fruit rings in half horizontally and place one red and one green half on top of marshmallows. Top marshmallows with red and yellow gumball halves. Place remaining green fruit ring half at bottom of button panel, top with a Smartie; cut a strip of licorice and wrap around the fruit ring.

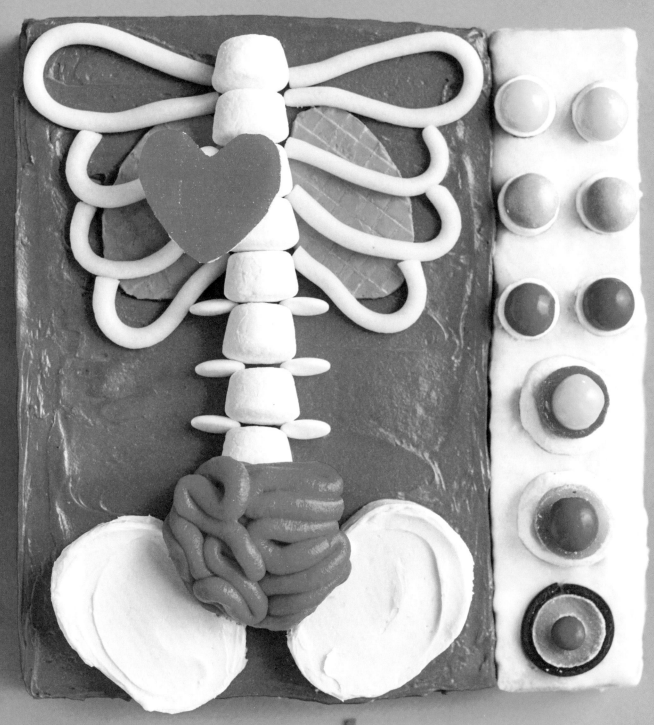

MAD SCIENTISTS

TAKES UNDER 1 HOUR

DECORATIONS

1-metre (1-yard) piece black licorice strap

12 flat-based ice-cream cones

150g (4½ ounces) white chocolate Melts

24 (70g) mini chocolate cream-filled biscuits

6 assorted coloured square jubes

12 pale pink candy-coated almonds

assorted coloured licorice twists

1 Cut licorice strap into 12 x 8cm (3¼-inch) long pieces. Trim ends on an angle to form a 3cm (1¼-inch) top and an 8cm (3¼-inch) base. Sit on inside edge of ice-cream cone.

2 Melt chocolate (page 113). Twist biscuits to halve; discard or reserve halves without filling for another use. Use melted chocolate to secure biscuits to licorice straps to make goggles.

3 Cut jubes in half, cut each in half diagonally to form triangles to make bow ties. Use melted chocolate to secure bow ties and almonds to ice-cream cones. Fill cone cavities with licorice twists for crazy hair.

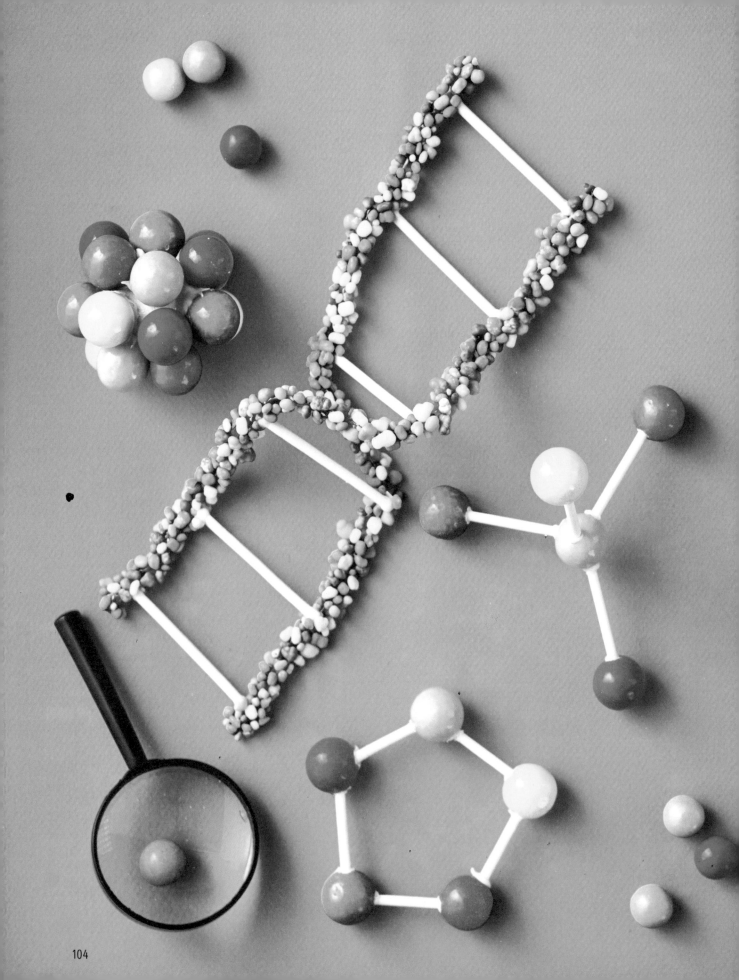

MOLECULE POPS

Each recipe makes 1 'molecule'.

ATOM BALL

TAKES UNDER 30 MINUTES (+ STANDING)

Melt 200g (3 ounces) white chocolate Melts (page 113). Use kitchen scissors to trim one giant white marshmallow into a sphere shape. Stick 18 gumballs to marshmallow using a little melted chocolate (allow time for the chocolate to set before attaching the next gumball).

DNA

TAKES UNDER 30 MINUTES (+ STANDING)

Melt 150g (4½ ounces) white chocolate Melts (page 113). Using kitchen scissors, cut 6 cake pop sticks into 6cm (2½-inch) lengths. Lay 2 nerd ropes next to each other; use chocolate to glue the ends of the cake pop sticks crossways onto rope. Leave until set. Gently twist strands into a DNA shape.

TEST KITCHENIUM MOLECULE

TAKES UNDER 30 MINUTES (+ STANDING)

Trim 4 cake pop sticks into 4.5cm (1¾-inch) lengths. Melt 100g (3 ounces) white chocolate Melts (page 113). Using picture as a guide and a small pointy knife, make a small hole into 4 gumballs. Make 4 small holes, on opposite sides, into a separate gumball for the centre. Dip ends of the cake pop sticks into melted chocolate; using picture as a guide, press sticks into gumballs to form a 3D molecule shape. Stand until set.

CARBON-BASED RING CHAIN

TAKES UNDER 30 MINUTES (+ STANDING)

Trim 5 cake pop sticks into 3.5cm (1½-inch) lengths. Melt 150g (4½ ounces) white chocolate Melts (page 113). Using picture as a guide, make small holes into 5 gumballs. Dip each end of cake pop sticks into melted chocolate; press sticks into gumballs to form a 5-sided molecule bond. Stand until set.

OLD RICKETY BRIDGE

TAKES OVER 1 HOUR (+ STANDING)

EQUIPMENT

35cm x 45cm (14-inch x 18-inch)
rectangular cake board (page 112)

2 x 25cm (10-inch) wooden skewers

CAKE

1½ x 453g (14½-ounce) tubs vanilla
frosting

blue and royal blue food colouring

1 x 450g (14½-ounce) packaged
double unfilled sponge cake slabs

3 muffins or cupcakes, uniced

4 mini cupcakes, uniced

DECORATIONS

375g (12 ounces) milk chocolate Melts

50 pretzel sticks

2 x 30cm (12-inch) pieces black
licorice bootlace

5 apple licorice twists

1 white meringue kiss, crushed

5 fun-size chocolate-coated
honeycomb

2 choc-vanilla mallow bites

7 brown M&M's

1 Tint 2 tablespoons of the frosting light blue; tint remaining frosting royal blue.

2 Secure one cake to cake board with a little royal blue frosting; spread top and sides of cake with frosting (you only need one cake slab for this recipe; discard or keep the remaining cake for another use). Use lighter blue frosting and a spoon to swirl small 'waves' over the cake.

3 Melt chocolate (page 113). Reserve ¼ cup melted chocolate. Place muffins and cupcakes together in two clusters on a sheet of baking paper to make 'rocks'; spoon chocolate over muffins to coat. Stand for 10 minutes or until chocolate sets. Position rock clusters opposite each other on long sides of cake (they should be far enough apart to hold bridge).

4 To make bridge, place skewers side by side 5cm (2 inches) apart. In small sections, brush skewers with reserved melted chocolate and secure pretzel sticks across skewers, leaving 2cm (¾-inch) of skewer exposed at each end. Stand for 10 minutes or until chocolate sets.

5 Perch bridge on top of rock clusters and use a little chocolate to cover exposed skewer ends and secure to rocks. Using melted chocolate, secure one pretzel stick upright to the rock on each corner of the bridge and 2 in the centre, trimming to size if required. Stand for 10 minutes or until chocolate sets. Wrap licorice bootlace around each side of bridge with a little melted chocolate to secure. Hold in place until chocolate sets.

6 Cut thin strips into one end of the apple licorice, without cutting all the way through. Place around the rock clusters, using melted chocolate to secure if necessary. Sprinkle crushed meringue on and around the 'water'. Arrange honeycomb, mallow bites and M&M's along the water's edge.

TIP *Start this recipe the day before to give the jelly time to set; simply cut into cubes on the day of the party.*

SQUARE-CUT GEMSTONES

TAKES OVER 1 HOUR (+ REFRIGERATION)

EQUIPMENT

two 20cm x 30cm (8-inch x 12-inch) lamington pans

cooking-oil spray

3-litre (12-cup) baking dish 5cm deep x 23cm wide x 33cm long (2-inches x 9¼-inches x 12¾-inches)

JELLY

4 x 85g (3-ounce) packets different flavoured jelly (we used raspberry, berry blue, lemon and purple grape)

4 teaspoons gelatine powder, plus ½ cup (80g) extra

1.5 litres (6 cups) milk

395g (12½-ounce) canned condensed milk

1 Lightly spray lamington pans with oil. Prepare 2 jelly flavours according to packet instructions adding an additional teaspoon of gelatine to each packet of jelly crystals; pour one colour into each pan. Refrigerate for 3 hours or until set.

2 When the jelly is set, prepare the remaining 2 flavours according to packet instructions adding an additional teaspoon of gelatine to each packet of jelly crystals; cool to room temperature. Pour one colour on top of each set jelly. Refrigerate for 3 hours or until set.

3 Bring milk and condensed milk to just below boiling point in a large saucepan, stirring until combined. Remove pan from heat. Whisk extra gelatine into milk mixture until gelatine is dissolved.

4 Grease and line baking dish with plastic wrap pressing well to avoid air bubbles. Pour milk jelly into baking dish; cover surface with plastic wrap to avoid forming a skin. Cool to room temperature.

5 Turn one fruit jelly out onto a chopping board. Cut into 2cm (¾-inch) squares. Scatter coloured jelly squares over milk jelly. Repeat with remaining fruit jelly.

6 Cover surface of milk jelly mixture with plastic wrap. Refrigerate for 4 hours or overnight until set. Remove plastic wrap; trim edges, cut into cubes to serve.

BOUQUET OF FRUIT FLOWERS

TAKES UP TO 1 HOUR

EQUIPMENT

1cm (½-inch), 2cm (¾-inch), 3.5cm (1½-inch) and 5cm (2-inch) round cutters

25 rubber bands

25 x 25cm (10-inch) long wooden skewers

greaseproof paper or baking paper

small vase

DECORATIONS

1kg (2-pound) seedless watermelon

1kg (2-pound) rockmelon

1kg (2-pound) honeydew melon

3 kiwifruit (255g)

125g (4 ounces) raspberries

125g (4 ounces) small strawberries

1 Slice watermelon, rockmelon and honeydew melons into 1cm (½-inch) thick slices. Using the cutters, cut melons into assorted sizes. Peel kiwifruit; cut into 5mm (¼-inch) thick slices. Cut green hulls from strawberries.

2 Twist a rubber band securely around each skewer, 3cm (1¼-inches) from the top of the skewer (this stops the fruit from sliding down the skewer). Thread a combination of fruit onto each skewer, finishing with a berry or small slice of melon.

3 Wrap a small bouquet of skewers in greaseproof paper. Place in a vase to serve.

step-by-step
TECHNIQUES

Levelling cakes Many cakes need to have their domed tops cut off so that the cakes sit flat on a cake board or plate. Use a large sharp serrated knife to do this.

Preparing to decorate Many cakes are turned top-side down or cut-side down for decorating, though some are decorated top-side up for a domed effect. The recipe will indicate if the cake is to be turned upside down to decorate.

Cutting cake into layers (1) Use wooden skewers as a guide for the knife to split the cake. If the cake is large, long skewers can be pushed through the cake, from one side to the other.

Cutting cake into layers (2) If the cake is small, use toothpicks to mark the layer. Use a sharp serrated knife to split the cake. Cut the cake just above the skewers or toothpicks, you should feel the knife touch the skewers as you cut through the cake.

Coating the side of a cake Have the ingredient to coat the cake in a large shallow pan – this can be coconut, hundreds and thousands or nuts, etc. Hold the cake between both hands and roll the cake like a wheel to cover the frosting.

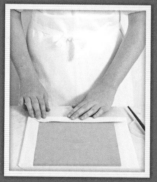

Covering a rectangular/square cake board Cut the covering paper about 5cm (2 inches) larger than the board; place the board, top-side down, on the back of the paper. Use tape or glue to stick the paper to the board. Glue a piece of paper to the back of the board to neaten the appearance, if you like.

Covering a round cake board (1) Cut the covering paper about 5cm (2 inches) larger than the board, and place the board, top-side down, on the back of the paper. Snip the paper border, on an angle, all the way around.

Covering a round cake board (2) Fold each snipped piece of paper over onto the board; tape or glue the paper onto the board. Glue a piece of paper to the back of the board to neaten the appearance, if you like.

To make small chocolate curls
Slightly warm a block of chocolate between your hands; drag the blade of a sharp vegetable peeler evenly down the side. For larger curls, run the blade of a cheese slicer down the back of the chocolate.

Melting chocolate Place in a medium heatproof bowl over a medium saucepan of simmering water, making sure that the water in the pan doesn't touch the bottom of the bowl or the chocolate will overheat and seize (turn hard and grainy). Stir until the chocolate is melted then remove from the heat.

Colouring chocolate Once melted, add a drop or two of colour to the chocolate. Use a colouring that's suitable for chocolate, as these don't 'seize' chocolate like water-based ones tend to do. If tinting a pastel colour, food colourings from supermarkets are fine as you only need a little; for darker more bold colours use gel or oil-based pastes.

Piping chocolate Half-fill a paper or disposable piping bag with melted chocolate. Fold the top of the bag over to enclose the chocolate. Cut a tiny tip off the end of the bag; test to see if it is large enough for the piping you are doing, if not, carefully cut the hole a little larger.

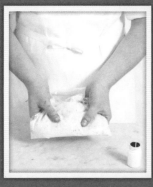

Colouring sugar or coconut Place the sugar (or coconut) in a small ziptop bag, and add a few drops of food colouring. Massage the colouring into the sugar/coconut until it is evenly coloured. Add the colouring a drop at a time, until you get the depth of colour that you want.

Making a paper piping bag (1) Cut a square from a sheet of baking paper, fold it in half diagonally, then cut it in half along the fold to make two equal-sided triangles.

Shaping the paper piping bag (2) Hold the apex of the triangle towards you, wrap one point of the triangle around to form a cone shape; repeat with the other point, then wriggle the three points of the triangle until they line up perfectly.

Securing the paper piping bag (3) Staple the bag to hold the three points of the triangle in place. To use, half-fill the bag with icing or melted chocolate, snip a tiny piece from the point of the bag, and pipe a little icing to see if the hole is large enough, if not, snip a little more from the point of the bag.

DRAVIDO DINOSAUR PAGE 85

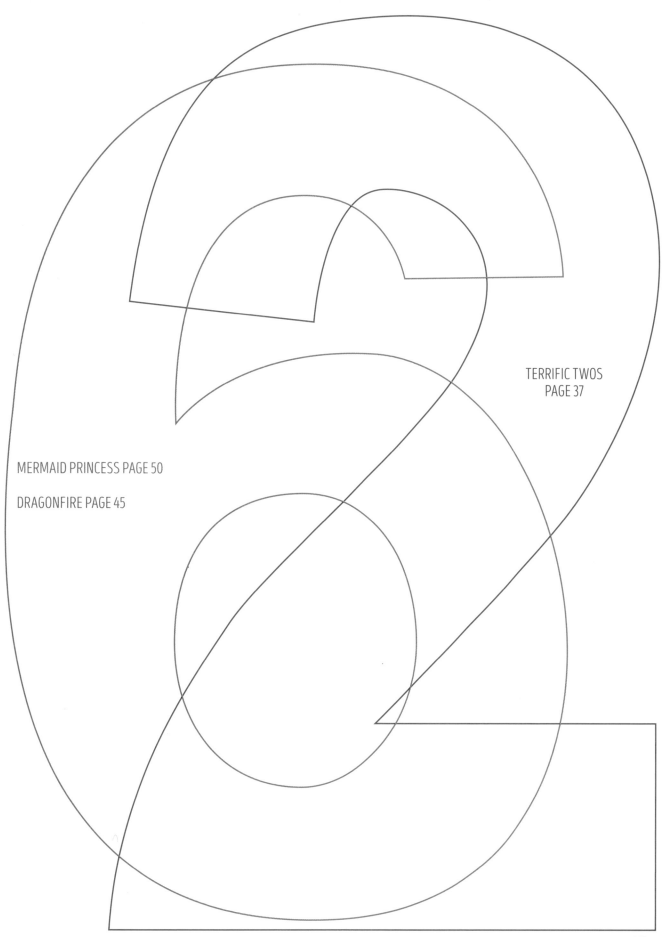

GLOSSARY

BAKING PAPER (parchment paper or baking parchment) a silicone-coated paper primarily used for lining baking pans and trays so cakes and biscuits won't stick, making removal easy.

BISCUITS also known as cookies.

CACHOUS also known as dragées; these minuscule (3mm to 5mm) metallic-looking-but-edible confectionery balls are available in silver, gold or various colours.

CAKE BOARDS often made from masonite and covered in a thick non-absorbable paper, silver or gold coloured. Come in myriad sizes, usually round or square. If displaying on a cake board, rather than a plate, the board is often 10-15cm larger than the cake, so it can be lifted and transported without fingers poking holes in the icing. The remaining cakes are placed on cake boards of the same size. If displaying on a cake plate, the base board should be the same size as the cake (see 'Covering a Cake Board, page 112).

CHOCOLATE

choc Bits also known as chocolate chips and chocolate morsels; available in milk, white and dark varieties.

dark eating also known as semi-sweet or luxury chocolate; made of a high percentage of cocoa liquor, cocoa butter and a little added sugar.

Melts small discs of compounded milk, white or dark chocolate; these are ideal for melting and moulding as they tend to hold their shape.

milk mild and very sweet; similar in make-up to dark with the difference being the addition of milk solids.

white contains no cocoa solids but derives its sweet flavour from cocoa butter. Very sensitive to heat so watch carefully when melting.

COCOA POWDER also known as cocoa; dried, unsweetened, roasted and ground cocoa beans (cacao seeds).

dutch cocoa treated with an alkali to neutralise its acids. It has a reddish-brown colour, a mild flavour and is easy to dissolve in liquids.

COCONUT

desiccated dried, finely shredded coconut.

essence produced from coconut flavouring, oil and alcohol.

flaked dried, flaked coconut flesh.

shredded strips of dried coconut.

FOOD COLOURING dyes used to change the colour of foods.

concentrated pastes or gels, which is what we used throughout this book, are the easiest to use, although a little more expensive.

liquid dyes the strength varies depending on the quality. Useful for pastel colours only, as adding large amounts of liquid colouring will break down most icings. Also useful for painting icing sculptures.

powdered colourings are best for primary colours or black.

FRIED NOODLES crispy egg noodles packaged (commonly a 100g packet) already deep-fried.

FRECKLES chocolate buttons coated on one side with coloured hundreds and thousands (nonpareils).

HUNDREDS AND THOUSANDS also known as nonpareils; tiny sugar-syrup-coated sugar crystals that come in a variety of bright colours and are used to decorate cakes.

ICE-CREAM we use full-cream ice-cream.

cones cone-shaped crisp sweet biscuit used for serving ice-cream; we used both flat-bottomed and pointy-ended cones.

wafers crisp rectangular biscuits used to serve with ice-cream.

JAM also known as preserve or conserve; most often made from fruit.

JAM ROLLETTES also known as sponge rollettes, filled with jam or jam and cream; we use jam-filled rollettes without the cream.

JELLY CRYSTALS a powdered mix of gelatine, sweetener and artificial fruit flavouring that's used to make a moulded, translucent, quivering dessert. Also known as jello.

JUBES sugar-coated fruit-flavoured sweets.

LICORICE an aniseed-flavoured sweet that comes in straps, tubes and ropes.

allsorts layered sweets consisting of licorice and fondant.

LIFESAVERS round hard sweets with a hole in the centre; also known as polo mints.

LOLLIPOP a boiled sweet on a stick.

LOLLY/LOLLIES confectionery also known as sweets or candy.

MARSHMALLOWS a light, airy sweet that holds its shape. Made from sugar, glucose, gelatine and cornflour.

METAL SPATULA also known as a palette knife. Come in small, medium and large. The larger ones have flexible steel blades. There are two types, straight-bladed, and offset or crank, which is used for getting into tight areas the flat straight blade can't. Spatulas are excellent tools for icing cakes.

SPRINKLES coloured cake sprinkles (nonpareils).

chocolate chocolate-flavoured cake sprinkles (vermicelli) or nonpareils.

SWEETENED CONDENSED MILK milk from which 60% of the water has been removed; the remaining milk is then sweetened with sugar.

SUGAR

icing also known as confectioners' sugar or powdered sugar; granulated sugar crushed together with a small amount of cornflour, which stops the sugar from clumping.

pearl also called nib or hail sugar; a product of refined white sugar, it is very coarse, hard, opaque white, and doesn't melt during baking. Available from specialist food stores.

pure icing this sugar is also known as confectioners' sugar or powdered sugar, but it has no cornflour added; this means it is very lumpy and it has to be sifted well before use.

VANILLA EXTRACT obtained from vanilla beans infused in water. Vanilla essence, or imitation vanilla extract, is not a satisfactory substitute for pure vanilla extract.

INDEX

MORE COOKBOOK TITLES

you won't want to miss...

AVAILABLE FROM SELECTED NEWSAGENTS, SUPERMARKETS AND WWW.AWWCOOKBOOKS.COM.AU

ONLY $14.95

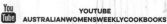

This book is published in 2016 by Octopus Publishing Group Limited based on materials licensed to it by Bauer Media Books, Australia. Bauer Media Books is a division of Bauer Media Pty Limited, 54 Park St, Sydney; GPO Box 4088, Sydney, NSW 2001, Australia phone (+61) 2 9282 8618; fax (+61) 2 9126 3702 www.awwcookbooks.com.au

BAUER MEDIA BOOKS

Publisher Jo Runciman

Editorial & food director Pamela Clark

Director of sales, marketing & rights Brian Cearnes

Creative director & designer Hannah Blackmore

Editor Wendy Bryant

Food editor Louise Patniotis

Operations manager David Scotto

Published and distributed in the United Kingdom by

Octopus Publishing Group Ltd

Carmelite House

50 Victoria Embankment

London, EC4Y 0DZ

United Kingdom

info@octopus-publishing.co.uk;

www.octopusbooks.co.uk

Printed by Leo Paper Products Ltd, China.

International foreign language rights

Brian Cearnes, Bauer Media Books bcearnes@bauer-media.com.au

A catalogue record for this book is available from the British Library.

ISBN: 9781909770362 (paperback)

© Bauer Media Pty Limited 2016

ABN 18 053 273 546